CONCILIUM

CONCILIUM
ADVISORY COMMITTEE

Gregory Baum	Montreal/QC. Canada
José Oscar Beozzo	São Paulo, SP Brazil
Wim Beuken	Louvain, Belgium
Leonardo Boff	Petrópolis, Brazil
John Coleman	Los Angeles, CA. USA
Norbert Greinacher	Tübingen, Germany
Gustavo Gutiérrez	Lima, Peru
Hermann Häring	Tübingen, Germany
Werner G. Jeanrond	Oslo, Norway
Jean-Pierre Jossua	Paris, France
Maureen Junker-Kenny	Dublin, Ireland
François Kabasele Lumbala	Kinshasa, Rep. Dem. Congo
Nicholas Lash	Cambridge, UK
Mary-John Mananzan	Manila, The Philippines
Alberto Melloni	Reggio, Emilia Italy
Norbert Mette	Münster, Germany
Dietmar Mieth	Tübingen, Germany
Jürgen Moltmann	Tübingen, Germany
Teresa Okure	Port Harcourt, Nigeria
Aloysius Pieris	Kelaniya/Colombo, Sri Lanka
Giuseppe Ruggieri	Catania, Italy
Paul Schotsmans	Louvain, Belgium
Janet Martin Soskice	Cambridge, UK
Elsa Tamez	San José, Costa Rica
Christoph Theobald	Paris, France
David Tracy	Chicago/Ill. USA
Marciano Vidal	Madrid, Spain
Ellen van Wolde	Tilburg, The Netherlands
Johannes Zizioulas	Pergamo, Turkey
Regina Ammicht Quinn	Tübingen Germany
Hille Haker	Chicago, USA
Jon Sobrino	San Salvador, El Salvador
Luiz Carlos Susin	Porto Alegre, Brazil
Silvia Scatena	Bologna, Italy
Susan A. Ross	Berkeley/CA, USA
Solange Lefebvre	Montreal/QC, Canada
Erik Borgman	Amsterdam, Netherlands
Andres Torres Queiruga	Santiago, Spain

CONCILIUM 2019/2

Populism and Religion

Edited by

Thierry-Marie Courau OP, Susan Abraham,
Mile Babić OFM

Published in 2019 by SCM Press, 3rd Floor, Invicta House, 108–114 Golden Lane, London EC1Y 0TG.

SCM Press is an imprint of Hymns Ancient & Modern Ltd (a registered charity) 13A Hellesdon Park Road, Norwich NR6 5DR, UK

Copyright © International Association of Conciliar Theology, Paris (France)

www.concilium.in

English translations copyright © 2019 Hymns Ancient & Modern Ltd.

All rights reserved. No part of this publication may be reproduced, stored in a retrieval system, or transmitted, in any form or by any means, electronic, mechanical, photocopying or otherwise, without the prior written permission of the Board of Directors of Concilium.

ISBN 978-0-334-03153-6

Concilium is published in March, June, August, October, December

Contents

Editorial   7

Part One: World Situations

Populism and Religion in Bosnia and Herzegovina   14
MILE BABIĆ

Populism and Religious Nationalism in India   26
FRANCIS GONSALVES

The Nationalisation of the Central Islamic Reference Point:
Islam and Populism in the History of Turkey   37
DILEK SARMIS

Part Two: Analyses

Religious Populism: the New Avatar of Political Crisis   50
FRANÇOIS MABILLE

Masculinist Populism and Toxic Christianity in the United States   61
SUSAN ABRAHAM

Part Three: Challenging populism by theology

The 'People' of God and its Idols in the 'One and Other' Testaments:
How Sacred Scripture Challenges Populist Rhetoric   74
MARIDA NICOLACI

'Bridges not Barriers': The Potential of Christian Hope to
Counter Right-Wing Populism   89
ANDREAS LOB-HÜDEPOHL

Right-wing Populism and Catholicity: An Ecclesiological
Reflection 101
FRANZ GMAINER-PRANZEL

The Paradoxes of Populism and the Church's Contribution
to Democracy: Some Hypotheses 111
CARMELO DOTOLO

Part Four: Theological Forum

Summer of Shame: American Catholics and the Latest Wave
of the Abuse Crisis 124
CATHLEEN KAVENY

Listening to the Conversation: After the Synod of Bishops
Meeting on Young People, the Faith and Vocational Discernment 130
BRUNO CADORÉ

Contributors 136

Editorial

When does populism arise? In an existential sense, it arises when people think they are lost, they have lost or that they are on the way to lose dreams, benefits, statutes, positions, essential dimensions of their life, personal or group interests, often acquired through previous struggles or efforts, or when they feel personally endangered. Populism seems appear when there is a perceived crisis of living together in a pluralist context and/or when specific folks feel ignored by global political or economic systems. A nostalgia for an imagined past can creep in supplanting any effort to work towards a future for all. Groups close ranks defensively instead of opening up and welcoming others. Suffering, frustrations, worries, angers accumulate and intersect, backing one another. A sense of aggrieved injustice takes hold. Complaint becomes the mode of empowerment.

And 'saviours' emerge for these folks. Gifted speakers and manipulators of symbol and media systems easily exploit popular sentiments of fear and dis-empowerment. Pursuing the colonial principle of 'divide and rule,' manipulative leaders scapegoat segments of the population as the preferred strategy of social and political control using social media. Their arguments depend on the simplistic manipulations of binary categories of social and political division and simple vocabulary, cast as 'plain-speaking' leadership. Nevertheless, they are also prone to grandiose gestures of crudeness and violence, magnified many times, because these gestures are picked up by a sensationalism hungry media, catapulting them to even greater visibility. Consequently, such sensationalist and outrageous behaviour is perceived to belong 'to the people' in opposition to an elite, educated or wealthy group. The 'elite' are presented as ones who are corrupted[1] and far from the social realities of 'the people,' out of touch with the ordinary. In the outrageous and offensive challenge to the elites, a symbolic defeat of the elites is performed as a spectacle for television. Through the performance of outrageous offense, the populist leader presents as a credible alternative

Editorial

to the status quo. They present themselves as saviours of a national and global order by expertly referencing a golden past that can be resurrected and a golden future in which the status quo is unchallenged. Here, identity, religion and cultures become emotional touchstones. Forms of nativism, nationalism and identitarian politics are utilized in order to secure popular sentiment against the easily identified 'foreigners' and immigrants.

Religion in the hands of populists thus is of particular interest for theologians. Using religion to structure nativist and nationalist collectivity has been particularly effective in various parts of the world. This political power using religion draws on a traditionalist sense of historical religions as representing tradition, stability, and identity. Populist leaders thus succeed in managing and constructing religion and theological arguments by selectively focusing on specific doctrines, eliminating legitimate and peaceful religious leaders and solutions, sterilizing internal freedom.[2] Religion becomes the tool of the political leader with religious leaders receiving personal benefits.

Why is this issue important for today, for theologians? By analysing what happens in such situations, we can begin to understand how religions and religious systems are manipulated. Theologians need to investigate how religion is easily distorted and how populism co-opts religion. Studies of Christian[3] populism points that it is contrary to faith and doctrine and inimical to the life of communion and community. It also demonstrates how the institutional Church may inadvertently stand in the way of democracy. These complex theological issues, with repercussions for how we live into the vision of Vatican II requires robust theological analyses and arguments to counter the cheap distortions of populist religion.

This issue of *Concilium* approaches the topic from three broad perspectives. One is historical and descriptive, putting in view the process of using religion by populist leaders, with essays from different parts and religious contexts of the world. The second perspective is from religious sciences. It deepens the understanding of populism through an analysis of politics, economics and gender concerns. The third is a theological perspective, with studies intersecting with Scripture, political theologies, ethics, dogmatics, and ecclesiology to challenge populism.

The issue's framework and the first part of the description of world situations are opened by the Bosnian Professor of Theology and Philosophy

Editorial

at the Sarajevo Franciscan Theologate (Bosnia-Herzegovina), Mile Babić OFM, from his European experience. He addresses the question of populists' opposition in Europe to pluralism, freedom of thought, and the logic inherent to human rationality, preferring instead, arguments that are either *ad hominem* or *ad populum*. In response to them and to their insensitivity, he advocates a focus on the suffering of every other human being in the world as condition for culture and religious belonging. As he argues, articulating that aspect is a precondition of looking for the truth that will set us free.

The Indian Jesuit, Francis Gonsalves SJ, Dean of the Theology Faculty at *Jnana-Deepa Vidyapeeth* (Pune, India), and Theology and Doctrine Commission's executive secretary of the Catholic Conference of Bishops of India, analyses the many forms of populism that have mushroomed in India due to its complex diversity and size. He clarifies how current Hindutva religious nationalism and its tactics for manipulating history, symbols, and existential fears, is a populist movement with consequences for India's Hindu population as well as for its minoritized citizens. Hinduist traditions, poor masses, religious or subaltern minorities are really threatened by such populist politics.

Dilek Sarmis, a researcher at the *Ecole des hautes études en sciences sociales and Centre d'études turques, ottomanes, balkaniques et centrasiatiques/CNRS* (Paris), provides a reflection on the use of religion by populist politics in Turkey. She first presents a historical analysis of the initial republican decades which did not employ religious arguments or sentiments. In the present political context, however, she shows how religious identity is used for a massive remobilisation of Islam for cultural and identitarian motives by the current ruling party and country's president, and how with a such populist perspective, Turkish political values are being deeply transformed.

The second part of this issue, which focuses on social and religious analyses, begins with an essay by François Mabille, who is a Professor in Social Sciences, researcher with the *French Group Religions, Sociétés, Laïcités* (CNRS & EPHE, Paris), and general secretary of the International Federation of Catholic Universities. In the current world marked by deep social inequalities, crisis of political representation and questions of sovereignty, political parties proclaiming strong cultural and religious references recreate hard national identities bounded by rigid borders. The

Editorial

focus of Professor Mabille's essay hence, is the unexpected return of antiquated religious strategies in public and political spaces, in societies that formerly embraced secularism.

Professor of Theology and Postcolonial Cultures and Dean of Faculty at Pacific School of Religion (California, USA), Susan Abraham, explores the scholarly literature on Donald Trump's populist rhetoric that has been extremely successful with white Evangelical and Catholic American Christians. She argues that Trump's rhetoric subtly deploys the anxieties of white Christians and their sense of loss of privilege and power to reassert traditional and idealized views of masculinity and American citizenship. White Christians ignore Trump's outrageous public behaviour as satire because his displays of outrageous behaviour secures political power within the United States for them. Trump provides white American Christians with a believable figure of muscular masculinity, leaving them to express a specific form of patriotic and muscular Christianity.

The third and last part of the issue modestly challenges populism with theological arguments. Beginning with scriptural narratives, the first essay by Marida Nicolaci, teaching New Testament exegesis at *Facoltà Teologica di Sicilia* (Italy), shows how the modern phenomenon of populism can find parallels of the dynamics of identity building of the People of God in scripture. Questions of pluralism, alterity and differences, appear in these processes and in a constructive rereading of Christian scriptural materials. Such a way of reading scripture provides the way forward for an inclusive human society, fruitful for both individuals and communities, in contrast to the divisive promises of populist leaders.

Andreas Lob-Hüdepohl, Professor of Theological Ethics and Director of *Berliner Institut für Christliche Ethik und Politik* (Germany), provides perspectives from the Christian hope for building bridges and not walls. As Lob-Hüdepohl argues, such hope must arise from the concerns of the 'other' in any community. Populist behaviour, in contrast, tries by many ways to exclude those who are contesting such selective and divisive views of society, denying the fundamental equality of all peoples. As is well known, scare tactics using theologies of destruction and ending are manipulated to create fear and anxiety. Against these apocalyptical scenarios, Christian theologies of hope provide constructive theologies of community and relationship that are able to overcome the mental and social barriers standing in the way of a vision of a united planet.

Editorial

The Austrian Professor Franz Gmainer-Pranzl, of *Katholisch-Theologischen Fakultät der Universität Salzburg* (Austria), whose research focuses on intercultural philosophy and theology, specifically between Africa and Europe, wonders about the concepts of 'right populism' and 'catholicity' in a reading of *Lumen Gentium*. He argues that when a current populist religious argument conflates 'the true folk' to a 'Christian society', it functions as a strategy of myth production for political uses. His conviction is to create an alternative creativity to right-wing populist strategies, by appealing to a new 'courage to catholicity', i.e. for an optimistic orientation to the Gospel's force of liberation and realization in a world of diversities.

The Dean of *Facoltà di Missiologia* (Pontificia Università Urbaniana, Rome, Italy), Carmelo Dotolo, starts from the distortion engendered by and in our democracies which is manifested by a socio-political and cultural fundamental fracture propagated by populism. Facing this hermeneutical conflict and populism's intentionality in reforming the social framework on a local level, she looks to retrieve Church commitments able to stimulate democratic forces to neutralize populist and authoritarian leaderships. She promotes her public responsibility as 'People of God', through her care of an ethic of the community, of the relationship between rights and duties of members in serving their communities, of the praxis for dialogue between multiple cultures and religions, and of an economic framework attentive to integral ecology.

The theological forum addresses two contemporary events. The first paper goes back to last summer's revelations of sexual abuses in the US Church by the ethicist and Professor of Law and Theology, Kathleen Kaveny (Boston College, Boston, USA). The second from the Master of the Dominican Order, Bruno Cadoré OP (Rome, Italy), offers a reflection on the works of the last Bishops' Synod on Young People, their Faith and Vocational Discernment,[4] where he was the moderator of a francophone group.

Thierry-Marie Courau OP, Susan Abraham, Mile Babić OFM

Editorial

Notes

1. Cas Mudde & Cristóbal Rovira Kaltwasser, *Populism: A Very Short Introduction*, Oxford University Press, 2017.
2. Stefan Orth & Volker Resing (eds), AfD, *Pegida und Co. Angriff auf die Religion?*, Herder, 2017.
3. Walter Lesch (ed), *Christentum und Populismus*, Herder, 2017.
4. http://www.synod2018.va/content/synod2018/en/fede-discernimento-vocazione.html

Part One: World Situations

Populism and Religion in Bosnia and Herzegovina

MILE BABIĆ

Populism is present today throughout the European Union and throughout Europe, and nowhere more so than in Bosnia and Herzegovina. Present as a form of thinking, discourse and action, and present as a communication style, in politics, for sure, but also in everyday life. One might say it is present as both an ideology and a meta-ideology. The populist parties attract ever-increasing numbers of followers, while politicians of all stripes deploy populist patterns of thought at least sometimes. Consequently, populism is now the greatest threat to democracy in Europe.

In this text, I would like first of all to point out the meaning of populism. After that I would like to show to what extent populism was present in the former socialist countries by pointing to its deeper roots, its presence in the Middle Ages under a different name, fear as its basis and the democratic and theological answer to it.

I What is populism?

The German political scientist and professor at Princeton, Jan-Werner Müller, first lists and then describes the main characteristics of populism in his book, *What Is Populism*? According to Müller, that he be critical of elites is a necessary condition for a politician to be included amongst the populists, but not a sufficient one. Populists are anti-elite, but also always anti-pluralist, claiming they and only they represent the people. They declare anyone who does not think like them immoral and corrupt members of the elite (the elite is by definition immoral and corrupt). In their view, once they are in power, no opposition is legitimate. To empirically or rationally based objections that demonstrate the people are not 100% behind them, they vaingloriously insist that they alone are morally upright, and they alone represent the people as a whole.[1]

For Müller, populism is a form of identity politics that assumes only populists can determine what makes up the people's identity. In Bosnia and Herzegovina, we might put this as that only the populists can say who is a real Bosniak, Croat, or Serb, and who isn't. The populist claim is that the people they alone represent form a homogeneous totality, rather than a community of free and responsible individuals. Populists recognise no plurals: one people, one thought. Once in power, they strive to subordinate the state and its institutions to their own interests and, so, spread corruption and clientalism. They allow their clients and cronies free rein, which is why populist politicians tend to suppress civil society, as they cannot tolerate alternative opinion. They justify their suppression of freedom of thought on the grounds they alone represent the people. Their followers justify and defend them, if caught red-handed in corruption, on the grounds they are doing it for the real people. Populists are willing to change even the constitution, if required to head off the development of pluralism.[2]

The Croatian political scientist, Berto Šalaj, defines populism as a political meta-ideology with two core characteristics: the divinisation or deification of the people, and so the positive valuation of a united and homogeneous people, and anti-elitism. Šalaj situates populism between pluralist social systems of values, on the one hand, and monistic systems (like fascism, communism, and religious fundamentalism), on the other. In their book, *Dobar, loš ili zao? Populizam u Hrvatskoj*, he and Marijana Grbeša show that the sources of populism lie in representative democracy itself,[3] a position Jan-Werner Müller also argues for, qualifying populism as a corrupted form of democracy. For Müller, populists do not oppose the principle of political representation. They just insist they are the only legitimate representatives of the people. In a critical review of an essay collection entitled *Kršćanstvo i populizam. Jasne fronte?*, Axel Bernd Kunz stresses that populism should be understood as a debating strategy that is structurally closed-off to alternative opinions.[4] To put this more clearly, one might say that populists take democratic forms and procedures and fill them with antidemocratic content.

II Populism in former socialistic countries

When his book appeared in Belgrade in 2017, Müller took part in a public discussion with the historian Dubravka Stojanović and the sociologist Vesna Pešić. All three participants agreed that populism's crucial characteristic is anti-pluralism. Populists can't comprehend anyone thinking differently and consider those who do to be traitors, in the pay of foreign powers, merciless and corrupt. Noting that her own book on Populism the Serbian way would be out soon, Dubravka Stojanović pointed out in discussion that there has been populism in Serbia since the days of Svetozar Marković (1846-1875), the influential Serbian socialist thinker who represented the (leftist and Russian-inspired) Narodnjak form of populism and believed that the principality of Serbia would be able to skip several stages of historical development and pass directly from pre-capitalist forms to the socialist form of society, without needing to pass through capitalism. Nationalist populism in Serbia was further developed by Nikola Pašić (1845-1926), the founder and leader of the Popular Radical Party (Narodna radikalna stranka), by the Serbian Orthodox bishop Nikolaj Velimirović (1881-1956), who was both a Christian theologian and a Serbian National-Socialist ideologue, by Dimitrije Ljotić (1891-1945), a Serbian politician and Nazi collaborationist, and by Milan Nedić (1876-1946), the leader of the puppet government in Serbia under the Third Reich in the Second World War. Socialist self-management in the former Yugoslavia, under Josip Broz Tito (1892-1980), who served as president of the state with an unlimited mandate (i.e., for life), was a typical example of left populism. Prof Stojanović has shown clearly how both left and right populisms make their appeal to the people, whom they claim support them 100%, or even 104%, as did Slobodan Milošević (1941-2006), former president of Serbia and then of the federal republic of Yugoslavia and indictee at The Hague for war crimes. In populist politics, the ruling party equates itself with the people, the people with the leader, so that state = ruling party = leader. As a famous watchword in Serbo-Croatian from the Socialist era had it: Mi smo Titovi, Tito je naš ('We are Tito's, Tito is ours'). The leader of the Serbian radicals, Nikola Pašić, had earlier made a similar claim. Ultimately, Stojanović points out, populism, whether left or right, leads the country towards a spiral of violence in which that those who think differently are persecuted and killed.

The sociologist Vesna Pešić stressed that populism is a negation of democracy in which we find the maximum possible development of clientalism, as the individual must rely on the populist party to progress. Even when populists speak against elites, corruption, capitalism, et cetera, they are acting, she asserts, as standard-bearers of authoritarian forms of thought and action, not of freedom, as they often present themselves. She points out that the communist movement, whose leader appealed to the working people (class-based populism), and the nationalist movement, whose leaders calls on the Serbian people (nationalist populism), are both plainly advanced forms of populist system. In socialism, the true or real people was the working people, in nationalism it is the Serbian people. Both populisms ended in violence and wars with neighbouring peoples and states.[5]

It is worth recalling that all the characteristics of populism found in Serbia and mentioned by Stojanović and Pešić are also present and active – *mutatis mutandis* – in the other countries that emerged from the break-up of Yugoslavia and indeed in all former socialist countries. It is clear that anti-pluralism (which rejects alternative opinions as immoral and corrupt) appeals to the nation as an homogeneous totality rather than a community of free and responsible individuals, leads directly to hatred of the other and the different and, ultimately, to violence that seeks to destroy that other.

The nationalist parties within the Bosniak, Croat, and Serb peoples in Bosnia and Herzegovina are forever denying each other's legitimacy as representative of their respective constituencies. By indulging in this form of politics, they stifle human rights within their own groups. This fact alone is enough to show that not one of these political parties has any respect for human rights, the nationalist parties least of all. While claiming to support universal human rights, they are actually giving preference to national rights that are fundamentally particularist. As a result, national identity becomes more important than individual identity, no matter how clear it is to any politically informed person that there can be no democracy without freedom of the individual (citizen).

Populist politicians across Europe divide and polarise into 'us' and 'them', producing exclusivity and hatred and making easy promises they never intend to keep, in order to usurp and politicise government institutions and increase their own political power. They excoriate as immoral anyone who disagrees with them, deploying *ad hominem* and *ad populum* arguments and dismissing those based on the faculty of reason common to all human beings. It follows that such populist politicians are taking action against democratic institutions, objective reason, and fundamental human freedoms: the freedoms of conscience, thought, and speech. They appeal to the people and treat them as an homogeneous totality, a totality within which no one thinks for themselves, following their great and strong leader instead. They appeal to the voice of the people and to 'sound common sense', construing that voice and that common sense as made in their image and for their purposes. Apparently concerned for the ordinary man, their real desire is to increase their own power and pursue their own interests. They offer simplistic solutions to complex problems, because one (their) side contains exclusively the representatives of the real people (authentic and moral), while the other opposing side is made up of those who have betrayed the people, truth, and morality. They put themselves forward as the leaders who alone can save the people. They flatter and pander to the people (the *populus*), reinforcing the stereotypes and prejudices that already exist in the people and deploying them to their own purposes. They press only for their own interests, while insisting there is no alternative to them, they alone are the saviours of the people.

III Deeper roots of the populism

It now becomes necessary to say something of the deeper roots of populism. One of them is the crisis of democracy, which has caused a sense of insecurity. Democratic practice has clearly become remote from democratic ideals, equality between individuals undermined in the name of liberalism. The political centre and the middle-class are disappearing, to be replaced by two extremes: a group of the rich and powerful, on the one side, and a great mass of the poor, on the other. A certain erosion has taken place of social systems, like the communities in rural areas and smaller towns, in favour of the anonymity of life in large towns, which produces isolation, and of augmented globalisation, which has its winners and losers. In short, the democratic, economic, and social crises go hand-in-glove with a crisis in the culture, as recent waves of migration have reinforced fear of the other, particularly of those who are culturally and religiously different, specifically of Islam.

Political analysts and commentators have popped up in Europe to use every available catastrophe to spread fear of the other. In the place of trust in the other, they deepen distrust, spreading fake news and disinformation. It's important to note that the standard-bearers of populist politics have produced a profound polarisation (division) in society, and neither they nor the representatives of liberal democracy are prepared for or capable of two-way dialogue. The advocates of democratic values must be told they too bear a certain responsibility for accepting the populist logic that produces exclusion: either us or them – no compromise, no dialogue.

The prominent German sociologist, Ulrich Beck, talks of a global risk society (*Weltrisikogesellschaft*). He has developed an original theory of risk and reflexive modernity, in which he shows that the process of the individualisation of religion is itself ambivalent: it can lead either to religious fundamentalisms (closing in on the self) or to religious cosmopolitanism. For such religious cosmopolitanism, other religions are not a threat, but an enrichment. Anyone who integrates the religious traditions and perspectives of others into his own personal religious experience thereby knows more and learns more, not just about others, but about himself too. If we accept and value cultural and religious differences positively, then we enrich each other. The individualisation of religion, however, can produce fear in some, causing them to flee to religious fundamentalism for security's sake.[6] It is worth noting that European politicians have not resolved the fears and insecurities brought about by the ongoing processes of globalisation, modernisation, and individualisation, the deepening gap between rich and poor, and, especially, the suppression of democratic principles (equality and fraternity/solidarity). They have at best kicked them down the road. These fears have been intensified by the latest uncontrolled wave of migration and the populists are now projecting the sum of all these fears and securities onto refugees from non-European countries, as their new scapegoats.

The advocates of democracy answer populist bias with their own bias, painting the populists as suffering from a xenophobic disorder. This mutual rejection has resulted in violence, both on the European periphery and in the European centres (Paris, Brussels, Nice, Berlin, Munich, et cetera), causing states of emergency to be introduced out of this heightened sense of insecurity. It has also led to columns of refugees moving freely around the periphery and centres of Europe and so increased support for the populist parties, which have lost all faith in a united Europe, retreating and closing themselves off within their national states.

If we want to strengthen social democracy, then those who would fight for democracy must engage in dialogue with the supporters of populism, not discredit them with scorn. Populism is more than just a protest against corruption in the states of Europe or even against of the ruling elites. It is an expression of the great insecurity eating away at European society. Is the xenophobia to be found in the populist parties just an expression of their obsession with foreigners (immigrants) or of their need for help? How are we to reconcile the logic of the market and social welfare under conditions where the state shows an inability to assist the lower and middle classes? Those who feel socially and economically marginalised are looking for help and their concerns should not be ignored.

In their one-sidedness, populists exacerbate things in mobilising and amplifying popular dissatisfaction, fears, concerns, and resentments, using them for their own political purposes. The goal is to attain power, whatever the means: through easy promises, aping concern for ordinary people, feigning closeness with the people, and denouncing those who think differently from them as immoral. Populists themselves respect neither moral norms nor rational logic, and their argumentation always tends to the *ad hominem* or the *ad populum*. They are more concerned to impress the people than to arrive at any truth. They subordinate government institutions to themselves personally, allowing their clients or hangers-on to do whatever they like, under a form of special dispensation. Consequently, they care little for truth, morality, or social justice, their greatest concern being how to increase their own power. They glorify their leaders as charismatic figures above the rule of law, drawing on the assistance of religious populism to claim that those great leaders have been sent by God and that the voice of the people is itself God's voice. In this way, the desire for ever greater power is buttressed by divine legitimation (justification). One must, nonetheless, admit that the populists often ask the right questions, but give the wrong answers, as the then French Prime Minister Laurent Fabius put it in 1984.

IV Roger Bacon

Having studied the life and works of the great 13th century Franciscan thinker Roger Bacon, I have noted that what we call populism he termed errors and mistakes (*errores*) and obstacles to recognition of the truth on the path towards perfectibility and wisdom: 'the example of frail and unworthy authority, ingrained habit, the opinion of the ignorant crowd, and the cloaking of one's own ignorance with a show of apparent wisdom' (*fragilis et indignae auctoritatis exemplum, consuetudinis diuturnitas, vulgi sensus imperiti, et propriae ignorantiae occultatio cum ostentatione sapientiae apparentis*). The first obstacle to the recognition of truth is the following of frail and unworthy authority (in populism this is blind trust in the leader even when he is obviously mistaken, whether factually or morally), the second is the obstacle of ingrained habit (in populism this is reliance on stereotypes and prejudice), the third is the obstacle of uninformed public opinion (in populism this is the appeal to common sense and arguments made either *ad populum* or *ad hominem*). An *ad hominem* argument is an attempt to deny the truthfulness of a claim by drawing attention to negative characteristics or beliefs of the individual expressing it. An *ad populum* argument is an attempt to prove the truth of a claim on the grounds that many or most people believe it. The fourth obstacle is cloaking one's own ignorance in ways that present it as knowledge or wisdom.[7]

Bacon considered uninformed public opinion even more dangerous than reliance on unworthy authority or ingrained habit, 'because authority only solicits and habit binds, but public opinion gives birth to and confirms the obstinate [in their obstinacy]' (*nam auctoritas solum allicit, consuetudo ligat, opinio vulgi obstinatos parit et confirmat*). In his view, the proponents of error put their the faith in the multitude, as though a greater multitude were a proof of truthfulness (populists put their faith in the people as a whole, all of whom are on their side – *argumentum ad populum*). He also points out that the proponents of error expect to use the multitude to defeat those 'whom they could not best through reason' (*quem ratione superare non poterant*). Proponents of the third obstacle (uninformed public opinion) tend more towards violence and evil than proponents of the first two. All evil, Bacon says, that befalls the human race does so when people celebrate their errors (lies) as truth and their evil as good. The proponents of the fourth obstacle are of this sort: they care neither for truth nor good, any more than do today's populists.[8]

V Fear as basis of populist logics

The former British Prime Minister, Tony Blair, gave a very instructive answer to a question about the radical polarisation that has come about in European societies (with populists on the one side, their opponents on the other) in an interview given to the Zagreb newspaper, *Jutarnji list* (*Morning Press*), on September 2, 2018. He pointed out that 'populism exists on both left and right, partly as a result of economic factors, like the financial crisis, but also partly because of cultural factors, e.g. as a consequence of immigration' and that the solution lies in creating a strong centre. Blair also stresses the importance of listening and understanding 'why people choose populism, because, if we don't find answers to their sincere concerns and issues, then the process whereby the traditional political parties are being taken over by populists will continue and intensify.' The true threat to democracy is 'for the world to divide into two groups of people and not willing to listen to each other, to talk to each other, and so to love each other.' For him, the soul of democracy lies in 'a sense for compromise, getting along, and believing that what connects us is more important than what divides us.'[9] It is particularly dangerous to deny all legitimacy to things just because we do not agree with them.

The question now arises as to what degree religions have just made nice with national populism and to what degree they have actually supported it. The eminent Croatian historian and former professor of history at Yale, Ivo Banac has demonstrated in his book *Hrvati i Crkva* (*The Croats and the Church*) how the Catholic Church succeeded in resisting communism (Stalinism), whose programme required a dismantling of religion, along with scientific demonstration of God's non-existence, expressed in a new ideology called scientism. The Communist theoreticians thus advocated 'scientific atheism' (they declared it possible to prove in a scientific way that God does not exist).[10] The church became fully modern only once it had accepted nationalism as the height of modernity. One should perhaps add that the thesis of one's own people's infallibility has been given particular emphasis as sentences have been issued at the International Court in The Hague. None of the sides is ever willing to accept that there might be criminals amongst their people or to accept the verdict of the court, as those being condemned for the crimes they committed should rather be considered heroes, saints, and martyrs. It follows that the members of a given people are moral especially when committing war crimes, because it was for their people they did them. What Banac says of Catholicism is also true – *mutatis mutandis* – for both Orthodoxy and Islam in all the countries into which Yugoslavia dissolved and in the other former socialist countries more generally.

Looking at populism more closely, we may note that populist logic is built on fear. Fear (*Angst*) is, for Martin Heidegger, existential, integral to the very structure of the human mode of being, and may take on various forms, some pathological, under different influences. Such fear was intensified during the financial crisis in Europe (2007-8), which created crisis within the European Union itself. The refugee crisis deepened the crisis even further, as it struck at the foundational principles and values of Europe itself. Should Europe build its own stability and security on the exclusion of others? Or is a politics of openness and cooperation required? How are populism, terrorism, and the uncontrolled influx of refugees all to be resisted? From psychology, philosophy, theology we know well that the only proper answer to fear is trust. But, it must be trust that is not contrary to the logic of human reason.

VI A theological response to populism

What form might a theological response take to the fear and crisis so evident in populist politics? My personal preference for a theological response to the populism spreading throughout Europe and the rest of the world would be to give life to the theses of the eminent theologian and founder of the new political theology, Johann Baptist Metz, who also happens to have been one of the founders of *Concilium*. His theses call for a break with the evil in our past and advocate for the spiritual development of Christians as bearers of hope. The key concepts in his theological thinking are: *passio, compassio, memoria passionis, the authority of suffering, and the history of suffering*. The relevance of his theses in today's world is obvious, not least in the regions that once made up Yugoslavia and in the other former socialist countries, but perhaps most of all in Bosnia and Herzegovina. Metz stresses that all the major religions and cultures recognise the authority of suffering, that is the authority of people who suffer because they are exposed to injustice, hatred, or violence:

> There is an authority that is recognised by all the major religions and cultures: the authority of those who suffer. Respect for the suffering of others is a condition of all culture. To be able to talk about other people's suffering is the precondition for all demands for truth. As well as of the demand for theology and for any Christology.[11]

His first thesis sets out that all the major religions and cultures recognise the authority of those who suffer. This assumes that humanity and everybody who goes to make it up have a shared responsibility for all the suffering that takes place within humanity. There is, thus, a universal responsibility, which means that there can be no suffering in the world that does not concern us. Metz explains that this imperative derives from the universality of God's children. If we are all God's children (in theology) and if we are all equal (in politics), then we are bound to our responsibility for all suffering, not just by biblical tradition, but also by the principles of the modern democratic state. If we want to transform the world into a world of peace, not one of conflict, we must act on our responsibility for all the suffering in the world. This is a moral imperative enjoined upon us unconditionally, an unconditional command. It is from this reflexive awareness of all suffering, from this *memoria passionis*, that our hope in a better future grows, a future that is not a continuation of the evils of the past. The *passio Christi* and the *passio* of all humanity are inextricably connected. Jesus' first regard is messianic and directed primarily at the suffering of the other, at the suffering of each individual who suffers: 'whatever you have done unto even the least of my brothers, you have done unto me!'(Mt 25,40).

The second thesis posits that respect for the suffering of others is a condition for all culture. This is the criterion for distinguishing between savages and barbarians, on the one hand, and persons of culture, on the other. Barbarians and savages are those who do not respect the suffering of others. This barbarian can extend so far as actually enjoying other people suffering, the term for which is *schadenfreude*. When historians of culture discuss Europe, they refer to four cornerstones: Athens (Greek culture), Rome (Roman culture), Jerusalem (the Abrahamic religions), and the Germanic-Slavic peoples, who were barbarians and savages. This barbarism of the peoples (*gentes*) is evident throughout European history: during the Inquisition, during the wars of religion, during the Jacobin Terror, during the two world wars, in the concentration camps (the Holocaust and the Gulag) and in current technologically perfected forms of killing not just soldiers, but innocent civilians, women, and children. Today, what is being intentionally increased is the suffering of others, both qualitatively and quantitatively, rather than respect for that suffering. The words cult and culture share the same root, the Latin verb *colere, colui, cultum*, indicating that religion belongs at the very heart of culture. The common task of religion and cult is the perfection of human nature, not its destruction.

Metz's third thesis states that talking about the pain of others and articulating their pain is a precondition for seeking truth. Those who remain silent about the pain of others have no desire for learning the truth. They conceal that pain under a veil of silence, passing over the truth in silence, over what has truly happened. That is, they do not desire to know that truth which alone can free us from lies and error. In the former socialist countries, one side greatly exaggerates the number of victims, the other side grossly underplays it, showing clearly that neither side cares for the truth or for the victims.

VII Conclusion

Reflexive awareness of Jesus' suffering is subversive, as it leads us to a break with established understandings and inspires in us hope in a new future. Practical heirship to Jesus Christ has a mystical and political dimension, the 'open-eyed mysticism' (Metz), eyes opened to the suffering of others. With shared suffering (*compassio*) goes mutual address (*conversio*).

Translated into English by Desmond Maurer

Notes

1. J.-W. Müller, *What is Populism?*, University of Pennsylvania Press, 2016. In German: J.-W. Müller, *Was ist Populismus?*, Frankfurt am Main, Suhrkamp, 2016; in Serbian: J.-W. Müller, *Šta je populizam?*, Beograd, Fabrika knjiga & Peščanik, 2017. The Serbian edition was used in writing paper, especially p. 30-35.
2. Ibid., p. 15, 97-98.
3. B. Šalaj & M. Grbeša, *Dobar, loš ili zao? Populizam u Hrvatskoj (Good, Bad or Evil? Populism in Croatia)*, Zagreb, Tim Press, 2018.
4. See A.B. Kunz, „Potential und Versuchung", *Concilium* (German edition) 54 (2018) 3, p. 351, review of W. Lesch (ed.): *Christentum und Populismus. Klare Fronten?*, Freiburg im Breisgau, Herder, 2017 5. https://www.youtube.com/watch?v=nhYTixvylcY&t=1032s
6. U. Beck, *Der eigene Gott. Friedensfähigkeit und Gewaltpotential der Religionen*, Frankfurt am Main und Leipzig, Verlag der Weltreligionen, 2008, p. 209-237.
7. *The Opus maius of Roger Bacon*, 1-3, ed. John-Henry Bridges, Oxford, 1897-1900, I, p. 2, 9.
8. Ibid., p. 10-11.
9. Ibid., p. 10-11.
10. I. Banac, *Hrvati i Crkva. Kratka povijest hrvatskog katoličanstva u modernosti*, Sarajevo-Zagreb, Svjetlo riječi & Profil, 2013, p. 153-156.
11. J.B. Metz, *Mystik der offenen Augen*, Freiburg-Basel-Wien, Herder, 2011, str. 156.

Populism and Religious Nationalism in India

FRANCIS GONSALVES

Given its immense size and complex diversity, many forms of populism have mushroomed in India. Today, the populism of Hindutva religious nationalism is assuming virulent avatars that not only threaten democratic processes, but are also an affront to true Hinduism and an obstacle to the integral development of India's poor masses. By resorting to tactics like historicizing myths, mythicizing history, manipulation of symbols, labelling of its imagined enemies, and with support from the corporate world, the media and muscle men, the Hindutva lobby is striving to usher in a Hindu Rashtra, which can spell doom for the religious minorities and subaltern communities. Here, ultimate victory lies with the common wo/man whose wisdom has unfailingly seen through anti-people policies and will hopefully choose democracy over narrow religious nationalism.

I Introduction

Five decades ago, Ionescu and Gellner wrote: 'A spectre is haunting the world today: populism'.[1] Today, this spectre of populism – directed by India's Prime Minister Narendra Modi and driven by militant Hindutva – poses serious threats to Indian democracy. Aided by alliances of the Hindu Right, collectively known as the Sangh Parivar and led by the Rastriya Swayamsevak Sangh (RSS),[2] Modi assumed power in May 2014 after a landslide victory of his Bhartiya Janata Party (BJP), which boasts about performing even better at the 2019 polls.

In his *What is Populism?* Müller proposes that, for one to be labelled 'populist' one must: (a) be critical of elites; (b) be anti-pluralist; (c) claim to be distinctly moral while trying to prove one's competitors as corrupt;

and (d) play exclusionary forms of identity-politics. Moreover, populist governments usually: (i) attempt to hijack the state apparatus, (ii) strive for 'mass clientelism' and (iii) suppress civil society.[3] Based on these criteria, this article will analyse the politics and policies of Narendra Modi and allies to disclose the nature of Hindutva populism and to assess its success. It will also strive to show how the democratic structures which have been built over centuries by all Indians are steadily being subverted by right-wing nationalists today.

II Historiography in India: Waging War for a Pristine Past

Historiography is a useful weapon to prove antiquity and legitimacy to subjugate others. In his *The History of British India* James Mill's naïve periodization of India in terms of Hindu civilization, Muslim civilization and the British period, long helped Hindu fanatics to hold that the Muslims and the British (Christians) are guilty of destroying an ancient, monolithic, golden, Hindu epoch. This sense of hurt and loss was intensified when a Brahmin, Keshav Baliram Hegdewar, founded the RSS in 1925. Brahminic ideologues V.D. Savarkar and M.S. Golwalkar further fanned RSS flames with an exclusivist Hindutva ideology, with its own Constitution to restore lost Hindu pride and saffron flag distinct from the Indian tricolor.[4] Citing its concern solely about sociocultural issues, the RSS distanced itself from the unified Quit-India non-violent movement directed against the colonial powers. Moreover, its members were antagonistic to anyone working for a united, pluralistic India. This led embittered Godse to assassinate M.K. Gandhi in January 1948, for Gandhi's idea of India—respecting all creeds and upholding equality of all communities—firmly critiqued its Hindutva counterpart.

Contrary to the exclusivist and Hindu-hegemonic history, eminent historians like Thapar have argued that community configurations and cohesion in the Indian subcontinent were determined by location, language, occupation and caste, none of which were necessarily bound together by a common religious identity.[5] The battle against the colonial powers was undoubtedly a united, concerted one, involving all believers and unbelievers alike, who collaboratively built Independent India. B.R. Ambedkar, a Dalit (former untouchable), was the chief architect of the Indian Constitution, which guaranteed 'reservations' (affirmative action) for disadvantaged sections of society like the Dalits and Adivasis (tribals), as well as 'minority rights' for communities that could become victims of majoritarian agenda. Thus, 'religious minorities' like the Muslims and Christians were guaranteed Constitutional rights to freely practise and propagate their religion.

To ensure the continued success of the Hindutva historical project, public passions have been kept aflame by persistent efforts to mythicize history and historicize myths. The contributions of freedom-fighters like M.K. Gandhi, B.R. Ambedkar, J. Nehru and Maulana Azad, who spearheaded India's independence struggle and proposed projects for a unified, progressive, post-independence India, are at best eclipsed, and, at worst, these patriots are depicted as anti-national, pseudo-secularists, directionless, elitist or pro-Muslim (thus, anti-Hindu). By contrast, Hindutva ideologues like Savarkar and Golwalkar are extolled for their glorious visions of a Hindu Rashtra. Furthermore, obscurantist historians like Dina Nath Batra have been deputed to produce textbooks mixing history and myth, claiming that Ancient Bharat was unparalleled in every field of science, aeronautics and surgery in Vedic times long before the West even dreamt of airplanes or plastic surgery.[6] Historians dismiss these narratives as fictitious, regressive and harmful for India's future.

III Symbolisms in the Construction and Destruction of India

Turning myth into history and history into myth is possible through clever use of symbols. Symbols are potent means to either construct or destroy community. Unlike texts and narratives that require verbal explanations to clarify issues, symbols unfailingly achieve their aim not only by moulding public opinion, but also by evoking strong feelings of attraction or revulsion – causing publics to run riot during communal conflicts.[7] The Sangh Parivar has carefully crafted some symbols to catalyse the Hindu nationalist cause. Among the most potent of these symbols are idyllic images of the Hindu Rashtra, Lord Ram's *janmabhoomi* (birthplace), holy cows, 'Jai Sri Ram' salutations, and attempts at universalizing the Bhagavat Gita, Gayatri Mantra and Yoga.

The December 6, 1992 demolition of the Babri Masjid – also claimed to be Ram's *janmabhoomi* in Ayodhya, UP – is arguably the most volatile confrontation that polarizes Hindus versus Muslims till today. With both sides unrelenting, the Indian Courts seem clueless on how to break this deadlock and arrive at a mutually-acceptable ruling. The Ayodhya rioting was followed by the Gujarat pogrom of hundreds of Muslims in February 2002, with Chief Minister Modi emerging as undisputed champion among Hindutva hardliners and the BJP staking claims to be trusted custodians of Hindu heritage and all Hindus, at large. The BJP's electoral successes in Gujarat were replicated in UP when in March 2017 Yogi Adityanath, Mahant (head priest) of the Gorakhnath Math, was installed as Chief Minister of UP. Known for his vitriolic tirades against Muslims and Christians, cow politics and *gharvapasi* (homecoming) controversies abounded.

Cow protection is a most contentious issue pitting the so-called 'upper-caste' Hindus who hold that cows must be protected at all costs, against many others of the so-called 'low castes' and creeds who not only eat beef but also subsist on the meat market: cow-slaughter, selling beef, export-import trading and leather industry. The ban on cow-slaughter gave reason to *gau-rakshaks* (cow protectors) to take law into their hands and lynch Muslims on mere suspicion of their possessing beef. Moreover, the major offensive of Hindu hardliners against Christians under BJP rule was in 1998-1999 in Gujarat's Dangs District, when Christian institutions, chapels and Adivasis were attacked allegedly for 'forcibly converting' Hindus to Christianity. In UP and Gujarat, many of those who converted to Christianity were forced to undergo purification rituals called *gharvapasi* (literally, homecoming), presuming, of course, that India's religious 'home' is Hinduism. In this regard, Hindutva maintains that, for enjoying full citizens' rights in the Hindu Rashtra, one must love the nation not only as one's birthplace (*janmabhoomi*) but also as one's 'holy land' (*punyabhoomi* or *pitrubhoomi*). With this caveat, Muslims and Christians are automatically denied equal citizenship with Hindus.

Modi himself is a larger-than-life symbol – quintessential *Purusha* of the emergent Hindu Rashtra: brave bachelor who has sacrificed all for the Rashtra, messiah of a wounded Hinduism, small-time tea-vendor who rose to fame by hard work, singularly focused on development, invincible at the polls, tough on terrorists, and unrepentant for destroying 'enemies' of the Rashtra. On Indian platforms, Modi's shrewd rhetoric, grandiose gestures, catchy slogans and emotive appeals mesmerise the masses. And, on his fifty-eight foreign trips from May 2014 till October 2018, he has greeted Presidents Obama and Trump, and Prime Minister Netanyahu not simply with protocolled handshakes, but with what seem like hugs between close friends, unapologetically gifting them copies of the Bhagavat Gita. Modi's élan makes many Indians proud and hopeful – awaiting those *aache din* (good days), which Modi always promises, yet, never produces in reality.

IV Do Define or Be Defined? Issues of Identity

While the Western mind prefers precision with 'either-or' categorization, Eastern mindsets are comfortable with 'both-and' descriptions. Consequently, given the diversity that characterizes India as regards culture, caste, creed and class, Indians feel at ease with myriad identity-markers. Not long ago, many Indian Christians would not object to being labelled 'Hindu-Christian' – i.e., Hindu by culture and Christian by religion. However, increasingly aware of the processes of assimilation and alienation that surreptitiously seek division and demarcation of who is Hindu/Indian and who is not, the religious minorities fear for their own identity and now desire to assert their right to decide 'who' they are, rather than submit to the 'tyranny of labels' and permit the powerful to decide 'who' they should be.[8]

Hindutva holds five 'Ms' – Marxism, Macaulayism, Missionaries, Materialism and Muslim extremism[9] – to be enemies of the Hindu Rashtra, each providing scope for labelling foes. Thus, historians like Thapar who propose pluralistic, progressive histories of India are dubbed 'Marxist'. Christians are projected as 'missionaries' who forcibly convert Hindus to Christianity, while Christianity itself is linked to 'Macaulayism' on account of the colonialists mostly being Christian and since Indian Christians manage many English-medium educational institutions. Likewise, Muslims are randomly regarded as 'terrorists' or 'extremists' since it is held impossible for any Hindu to be a terrorist—despite members of Hindu organizations like the *Sanatan Sanstha* being arrested for murders, bombings and possession of explosives. Given that Muslims and Christians account for just 14.2 and 2.3 percent of the Indian population, respectively, while Hindus account for 79.8 percent,[10] one wonders why Hindus are made to feel insecure and why efforts are underway to ghettoize the minorities. The Justice Sachar Report of 2006 even showed that the Muslims are among the poorest and most backward of communities in India.[11] So, all talk of Muslims surpassing Hindus not only numerically but also economically is pure eyewash.

Among the many identity-markers that continue being foisted upon those who allegedly threaten Hindutva populism are tags like anti-national, unpatriotic, *sickular*, pseudo-secularists, Marxists, Maoists, Naxalites, jihadis, foreigners, proselytizers, extremists, terrorists, and so on. Other appellations that subtly seek to deprive India's indigenous peoples their rights of affirmative action and land-entitlement are '*vanvasis*' (literally, forest-dwellers) rather than 'Adivasis' (original-inhabitants). Finally, media persons who express differences of opinion with Hindutva hardliners are called '*presstitutes*' (media-prostitutes) to show that their views are perverse, unoriginal and abhorrent to right-minded citizens who respect governmental authority and obey orders.

V Censoring Press, Stifling Dissent and Deifying the Leader
Today, Indian democracy faces grave threats to freedom of expression with the stifling of democratic dissent. Many local newspapers and TV channels in Indian languages have long been publicizing what is produced and peddled by the government. Yet, by contrast, many English news channels and media houses had retained their autonomy, respected democratic space and allowed viewpoints that differed from their own. This trend has changed, and an atmosphere of fear has paralyzed the Indian media. Eminent TV anchors like Prannoy Roy, Barkha Dutt, Karan Thapar and Ravish Kumar who have disagreed with government policies, have either been trolled online or abused and threatened with dire consequences, even death. Attempts have been made to penalize popular channels like NDTV. Globally-acclaimed award-winning authors like Arundhati Roy, too, have not been spared, being branded anti-national, rebel, Pakistani and Maoist. Rationalists like M. M. Kalburgi, Govind Pansare and Narendra Dabholkar, as well as courageous journalist Gauri Lankesh, were shot dead for being critical of Hindutva politics.

One of the most recent and blatant cases of intimidating organic intellectuals was a crackdown on five so-labelled 'Urban Naxals' suspected of having links with the ultra-left subversives of the state. Along with these, an 82-year old Jesuit priest, Stan Swamy, working with dispossessed Adivasis in the state of Jharkhand, was also arrested and cases under the draconian 'Unlawful Activities Prevention Act' (UAPA) were drawn up against them. All these accused are committed lawyers, writers and social activists who have the interests of India's poorest and most exploited sections of society close at heart. A saffron-clad Hindu social activist, Swami Agnivesh, too, was manhandled, had his robes torn and ribs broken simply because he speaks of abolition of caste, the equality among all Indians, and fights for the rights of the rural poor and landless labourers.

While stifling of dissent is one side of the populist strategy, the other side is the support given to select press-persons and TV channels to air majoritarian and governmental views. Arnab Goswami, probably the highest paid TV anchor in India, and his 'Republic Channel' are regarded as mouthpieces of governmental and majoritarian viewpoints. Besides shouting down ideological opponents during primetime debates, Goswami's Republic Channel also launched a witch-hunt, vainly trying to prove that the Vatican, colluding with Indian bishops was conspiring to subvert the Hindu revival in India. Pastoral letters of three Catholic archbishops of Delhi, Gandhinagar and Goa, asking the faithful to pray for the country, were interpreted as church strategy to defame Modi's good governance and pressurize Christians to defeat the BJP.

Notably, today, with the InfoTech revolution and the pervasive spread of social media, public opinion 'for' or 'against' anything or anyone can be effectively engineered. India's last general elections in 2014 were said to be 'India's first social media elections'. Modi and the BJP flooded social media—depicting the contest as a bout between two opposing 'political brands': commoner *chaiwallah* (tea-vendor), Narendra Modi versus elitist *shehzada* (prince), Rahul Gandhi of the Nehru-Gandhi dynasty; good governance versus endemic corruption; decisiveness versus tentativeness; discipline versus chaos; respect for religion versus pseudo-secularism; etc. There were allegedly brilliant computer-whizzes handsomely paid to manage the election campaign. Modi's BJP obtained an absolute majority in the Lok Sabha (House of the People) with 282 seats out of a total of 543, while the Indian National Congress – ruling for 55 out of the 69 years of India's independence – won just 44 seats as compared to the 206 seats it won in 2009. Electoral successes apart, Modi is one of the most widely tracked persons on Twitter attracting some 43 million followers worldwide. Surprisingly, Modi has never appeared in any TV interview or public debate. He is a one-way communicator; others listen and obey.

VI Unholy Trinity of Neoliberalism, Religious Nationalism and Militant Might

Amidst rapid changes that India is undergoing and against the rising tide of cynicism about the state of affairs in the country, one might ask: Why is this populist brand of religious nationalism still acceptable – even if not fully agreeable – to large masses of the Indian public? The answer seems to lie in the religious character of India and the psyche of most Indians, which has never really changed despite claims of India surging ahead as a global superpower. Though there has been a 'democratization of religion' with many more members of the so-called 'lower castes' assuming positions of power, the so-called 'upper castes' do not accept such changes, for they inevitably lead to loss of socio-political power as well as weakened economic status. The elitism permanently ingrained in the caste system persists; and problems seem destined to continue.

Roy rightly observes, 'India's freedom struggle, though magnificent, was by no means revolutionary. The Indian elite stepped easily and elegantly into the shoes of the British imperialists.'[12] With the overthrow of the 'big enemy', Britain, the anomalies of India's caste system and the inequalities of the rural-urban divide remained unresolved. Post-Independence, Jawaharlal Nehru's vision of a prosperous, modern India – with 'secularism' and 'socialism' eventually added on to the Constitution – propelled urban Indians upward, selfishly striving for the welfare of their own family, clan, caste or community. This was possible under the leadership of strong leaders of the Congress. However, M.K. Gandhi's reminder to Indians that 'the soul of India lives in its villages,' and B.R. Ambedkar's persistent demands for the 'abolition of caste' were forgotten in the struggle to satisfy personal desires.

The parties that have long opposed the Nehru-Congress brand of politics – namely, the *Bharatiya Jana Sangh* (BJS) from 1951 to 1977 and the BJP from 1980 onwards till date – were perceptive in forging a loose unity of the lower castes, along with those looking for some succour in religious revivalism. In the late 1980s and early 1990s, with the Congress dabbling in 'soft Hindutva' and opening out India's doors to neoliberal capitalists, many Indians were beginning to be disillusioned with the empty promises of the Congress. Meanwhile, the BJP sensed that its poll prospects lay in driving a wedge between the so-publicized 'elites' and 'commoners', reviving Hindutva agenda, and posing itself as the protector of the majority

Hindu religion against the 'pseudo-secularists' shown as appeasing the religious minorities. Gujarat became the 'laboratory of Hindutva' and the 'Gujarat model of development' – with generous subsidies to foreign investors and Indian corporates, with sops thrown in for local players – became exemplar of the new, strong India.

Today, neoliberal capitalists have joined hands with religious chauvinists; and with aggression from the military and protection by the police, they keep alive a state of siege and tension, thereby retaining a stranglehold over the poor. The unholy nexus of Brahmins, Kshatriyas and Vaishyas – priests, warriors, and merchants, who perennially have pooled resources to perpetuate their powerful reigns—seems to profit once again from sociopolitical and religio-cultural systems. This time, two more factors are additionally in their favour: (a) the Dalits and Adivasis who were mostly opposed to upper caste/caste dominance are now being subsumed into the system as and when deemed convenient, and, (b) the electronic and social media is providing unstinted support to transmit fake news, foster doublespeak, fudge facts and figures, and deify the populist leader. This explains, to a large extent, the success of Hindutva populism.

VII Conclusion

During pre-election speeches in 2014, Modi melodramatically pleaded with the masses not to elect him as minister but merely as a *chowkidar*, watchdog, to confront the corrupt, Congress culprits who had robbed the nation for long. He swore to right historical wrongs and to set India on the fast-track of progress. Such rhetoric led to winning many state and local elections. However, the BJP suffered a colossal electoral loss in the February 2015 Delhi Assembly elections to the '*Aam Aadmi* Party' (AAP, meaning, Common Man's Party) headed by Arvind Kejriwal. The main reason was that people had seen through Modi's empty rhetoric and failure to translate promises into concrete projects benefiting everyone. While the BJP engaged in negative tactics of pointing out the lacunae of AAP, Kejriwal and his supporters, spoke a language of the commoner, had the broom as its electoral symbol, and promised concrete welfare measures like cheap electricity, safe drinking water, better roads, speedy redress of woes, etc. – what India needs at present. He won.

The current anti-democratic, populist wave can only be countered by raising the consciousness of the public. Commoners as *chowkidars* must show, first, that despite all populist propaganda of *aache din*, no 'good days' have come; the common wo/man still suffers poverty, hunger, threats, eviction from home and land, etc. Second, although Modi and his allies constantly attack the Congress for being elitist, the BJP leaders are no less elitist – mostly belonging to the upper castes and classes, with minimal Muslim representation. Third, while Modi boasts about being unsullied by corruption, BJP ministers are guilty of land scams, money laundering, shady arms' acquisition deals, unpunished rapes, lynching, besides having criminal backgrounds. Modi himself was banned from entering the UK till 2012 and the USA till 2014 for his alleged complicity in the 2002 Gujarat genocide. But, his current post provides him with the immunity to freely travel worldwide. Fourth, the unholy trinity of neoliberal capitalists, religious fanatics and military-police muscle-men must be exposed for what they are: self-serving exploiters of the poor and powerless. Fifth, organic intellectuals – authors, philosophers, journalists, poets, theologians, media-persons, semioticians, filmmakers – must strive to expose the doublespeak, evolve new symbols, reclaim the democratic space which is constantly shrinking. All this will only bear fruit if the common wo/man's concerns are highlighted in public life and socio-political debates.

India has had many populist movements both, at the national and local levels. After Independence, at the national level, one can think of Indira Gandhi who reigned supreme over India with a much-publicized '*Indira is India, and India is Indira*' slogan. Riding a populist wave, and keen on single-handedly usurping political power, she manipulated the declaration of a state of Emergency spanning June 1975 to March 1977, which eventually led to her downfall. Hindutva populism is today being animated by one man, Narendra Modi, who has been building up his image with great support from the corporate world, the media and the many nationalist associations who seek the resuscitation of an imagined, glorious Hindu Rashtra. So far, the processes of mythicization of history and historicization of myths, as well as symbolizations, identity-politics and the forging of alliances among the so-called 'lower castes' have borne rich harvests. It's often said, 'Indians do not cast their vote; but vote their caste!' Be that as it may, one hopes that, ultimately, all castes will cast their votes in favour of democracy, not narrow religious nationalism, which alone seems to be the finest option for all.

Notes

1. G. Ionescu and E. Gellner eds., 'Introduction,' *Populism: Its Meaning and National Characteristics* (London: Weidenfeld & Nicolson, 1969), 1.
2. Hinduism is not synonymous with *Hindutva*, which is an exclusivist, militant offshoot of Hinduism propagated by fanatic Hindus seeking to build a theocratic 'Hindu Rashtra' (Nation). The *Sangh Parivar*—meaning, 'Family of Organizations'—refers to the conglomerate of Hindu nationalist organizations started by members of the RSS, the Rastriya Swayamsevak Sangh, meaning, 'National Volunteers' Corps'. Each wing of the Sangh Parivar has its own policies and activities within the broad Hindutva ideology. For example, the Bhartiya Janata Party (BJP) is the political wing, Vishwa Hindu Parishad (VHP) is the religious wing, Akhil Bhartiya Vidhyarti Parishad (ABVP) is the youth association, etc. For details see V.D. Savarkar, Hindutva (Bombay: Veer Savarkar Prakashan, 1969); also, J. Sharma, *Hindutva: Exploring the Idea of Hindu Nationalism* (New Delhi: Penguin Books, 2011).
3. See J.-W. Müller, *What is Populism?* (UK: Penguin Random House, 2017), 2-4.
4. See M.S. Golwalkar, *We, or, Our Nationhood Defined* (Nagpur: Bharat Prakashan, 1947); and, Bunch of Thoughts, 3rd ed. (Bangalore: Sahitya Sindhu Prakashana, 1996).
5. R. Thapar, 'Imagined Religious Communities? Ancient History and the Modern Search for a Hindu Identity,' *Modern Asian Studies* 23/2 (1989): 209-231.
6. https://en.wikipedia.org/wiki/Dinanath_Batra, accessed on 10 October 2018. Batra is an RSS ideologue-historian who has stoked many controversies by proposing many fanciful theories—for example, that plastic surgery was probably known in ancient India since Lord Ganesh had an elephant's head implanted upon a human body.
7. A.P. Cohen, *The Symbolic Construction of Community* (Chichester: Ellis Horwood Limited and London & New York: Tavistock Publications, 1985), 11-38, argues that community is constructed not so much by geographical proximity of members as much as it is by symbolic fields that either unify or divide people. See P. Bourdieu, *Language & Symbolic Power* (Cambridge: Polity Press, 1991), 163-170.
8. R. Thapar, 'The Tyranny of Labels', K.N. Panikkar ed., *The Concerned Indian's Guide to Communalism* (New Delhi: Viking, 1999), 1-31, warns against naively labelling religious communities and setting them in opposition to each other since religion was not as important in ancient India as it is today made out to be.
9. See S. Roy, 'On Hindutva and the 'Five Ms' that Pose a Threat to it', 2 December 2014, https://www.newslaundry.com/2014/12/02/on-hindutva-and-the-five-ms-that-pose-a-threat-to-it, accessed 10/10/18.
10. https://www.census2011.co.in/religion.php, accessed on 12 October 2018.
11. See for additional details on the plight of Indian Muslims, today: O. Anas, 'Indian Muslims between Exclusion and Political Populism,' *Al Jazeera Centre for Studies*' Report of 30 November 2016.
12. A. Roy, *Public Power in the Age of Empire* (New York: Seven Stories Press, 2004), 6.

The Nationalisation of the Central Islamic Reference Point: Islam and Populism in the History of Turkey

DILEK SARMIS

This article proposes a reflection on the exploitation of religion by populist parties in Turkey through an historical illumination of the first decades of the Republic, generally associated with the laity and a marked distancing from religion. This approach allows us to analyse the links between the reconfiguration of religion in various fields of political and intellectual activity in the young Turkish republic and the present day experiments by the party in power: these evidence a massive remobilisation of Islam as a significant indicator of culture and identity, modifying the topology of the major values of Turkish politics from a perspective of populism.

The political and analytical notion of 'populism' refers to various realities. It has been shaped in accordance with differing historical and national experiments. In its overall approach, it harks back to various events in political and ideological leadership that have placed 'people' in opposition to their governing elites. Within a context of the political exploitation of this opposition, more or less built from the protagonists' voices and forged by circumstance, various tools of identity have been deployed amongst which we find religion with its changing contexts and histories.

To this end, Turkey's past and present allow us to embark upon a reflection on the relationships that have existed between religion and the mobilisation of the related nationalist and populist points of view. For the purposes of the present article, by 'religion' we mean both practices and tools. The practices are those of individuals who are attached to an assumed faith or to a regional or national culture and which contribute to their sense of identity. The tools are intellectual and political. They are used by the protagonists in relevant areas of activity, (political figures and their networks: business, journalists and also universities and intellectuals – theologians, philosophers, writers) with the aim of creating discussions and theories relating to the individual in his political context, both national and cultural. We shall examine the history of Islam's place in Turkish republican politics, to bring light to the journey towards what is presently presented as a concomitance of forms of nationalism and Islamic politics.

I Republican Turkey

Let us bring to mind some key moments in the history of the Turkish Republic. The imperial rule of the Sultanate to which the Republic succeeded was overthrown in 1918. This gave way to the occupation of Istanbul by the foreign powers and to a war of liberation under the leadership of Mustafa Kemal – the future Atatürk – which culminated in the Treaty of Lausanne of 23 July 1923 which fixed the territorial boundaries of the new Turkey. This war swiftly became one of the founding myths of the new nation. The declaration of the Turkish Republic on 29th October 1923 led to a series of reforms that brought together the issues of revolutionary modernity with the handling of religion: the abolition of the Caliphate and the new constitution of 1924, the closure of the religious orders in 1925, the adoption of a civil code based on the Swiss model in 1926, the new penal code, the adoption of the Latin alphabet and the Gregorian calendar in 1928. These institutional reforms where accompanied by others highly charged with symbolic meanings applying to dress (the forbidding of the wearing of the fez and the adoption of western styles of dress and hats) and to given names.[1]

During the early pioneering years, the constitution was built around six concepts called the 'six arrows (*alti ok*)': in 1927, 'republicanism', 'populism',[2] 'nationalism', and 'laity'. To these were added in 1931, 'statism' and 'revolution'. These endowed the nation state with teleological principles supporting the single party system and the leadership cult developed around the figure of Mustafa Kemal, 'Atatürk', the father of Turkey, paternalistic and semi-divine, the arbiter of patronyms and the spirit of the age. The Republic quickly put in place an imaginary back history. The Turkish History Institute, created in 1931, built an ideological and messianic national narrative, borrowed in part from the work on Turkey by orientalists, whose references were anti-Islamic, avoiding any transitivity with the Ottoman empire, now totally rejected by the new State. A university reform launched in 1933 reorganised departments and led to a massive purge of lecturers appointed under the Ottoman rule and to the recruitment of German professors – including a number of Jews – who were fleeing Nazism. Theology disappeared from universities and intellectuals and those in higher education were invited to work in accordance with the single party ideology and in the interests of the Kemalist revolution. Religion was placed under state control. In 1925, the religious orders, strong binding elements in Ottoman society and places of potentially significant political activity were forbidden, preventing the sustaining of an alternative, uncontrolled, source of power. The Turkish laity consisted above all in a placing of religion under supervision, and not merely in a transfer to a private sphere: in reality the republican project had never implied, strictly speaking, that religion would disappear from socio-political life.

Historiography, just like the imaginary world created around this Turkish reformation, places great emphasis on the movement of Kemalist Turkey to secularisation and laicisation, sometimes wrongly interpreted as a departure from religion.[3] By way of contrast, one can see an insistence by present journalists and political commentators on Turkey on a 'return of religion', an 'islamisation', seen as accompanying, or explaining, the arrival in power in 2002 of the present AKP (*Adalet ve Lakinma partisi* – Party of Justice and Development) and which has subsequently regularly been re-elected. Considered in the early 2000's as the best example of a poitical party in a Muslim country that had developed a compatibility with European standards, it has now been for several years as controversial within Turkey as in Europe. The AKP government is now seen both as a populist political movement exploiting religion as a means of reinforcing its hold on power and as a tool of Islamic ideology. These two dimensions arising from the AKP's policies and which are drawn from two different political dynamics – the one utilitarian and the other ideological – are nevertheless able to rub along together depending on the sensitivities of those in the party. Contemporary analysts also readily see the AKP experiment as a breaking with the Kemalist experience.

II Kemalism and religion

However, and although certain AKP leaders assume there is a distance between them and the Kemalist laity,[4] some of the ruptures – in particular those which are institutional and symbolic – are worth reconsidering, nuanced within a historical re-evaluation of the place of religion in the Kemalist state. The range of debates and actions by the present government are drawn, in fact, from the nationalist heritage and the approach to political action developed during the course of the Kemalist period.

A recurring theme of Turkish history lies in the identification between modernisation and secularisation. The modernisation of Turkey is seen as being due to the cultural and epistemological change that brought the religious institutions into line. However, set against the widely held ideas of a rupture with Islam and in spite of the Republic's break with the imperial regime of the Caliphate pre-1918, it is worth considering that, beyond the republican break up of 1923, secularised discussions[5] about religion (*din*) and morality (*ahlâk*) continued. It is important to evaluate these as structures that bind society together. They were able, albeit non intentionally, to promote more contemporary views of 'Islam' as a socio-political model. Religion has not disappeared from the public space but everything relating to it has been placed under State supervision. This is where the reference points of religion are to be found and where they are being reshaped through their progressive *nationalisation*, which explains in part the ease with which the present government has been able to lean on religion in opposing former political regimes. It benefits from the extraordinary audience for nationalist debates in Turkey – a still young republic founded on the mythification of a war of liberation against the common external foe.

Nationalism works through various historical events. Already during the final decades of the Ottoman period, the Empire's loss of national territory prompted the envisaging of an alternative national identity to that derived from expansionist imperialism, through attempts by Ottoman reformers and young Turks. 'Turkism' and 'pantouranism' (union of Turkish peoples) propounded a switching of the pluri-ethnic identity of Ottoman citizens, occasionally tribal in Imperial provinces, for one that was Turkish. These proto-nationalisms promoted an ethno-cultural variant, either centred around Anatolia, or encompassing a central Asian area. Debates and links[6] developed in particular after the 1908 regime-changing revolution that

The Nationalisation of the Central Islamic Reference Point

placed the young Turkish reformers in power.[7] Multiculturalism, no longer operative within the context of the creation of an autonomous nation state and taking into account the territorial losses, (Bosnia- Herzogivna 1908, Rhodes, Libya and Albania in 1912, followed by Bulgaria and Crete – first Balkan wars, October 1912 to May 1913), gradually lost relevance. It disappeared to the profit of a State led standardisation, assimilating all citizens into one territory, one language, one political regime. The genocide against the Armenians in 1915, accused of forming a Russian fifth column, epitomised the extremes of tension around the question of the ethnic, territorial and religious unity of the country. What would the 'Islamic' character of the country become as a consequence of this ethno-cultural substitution? Over all, the Islamic identity was both founded in and subject to a Turkish 'super' identity.

From 1923, Kemalist nationalism parted company with Islam as a point of reference which, from then on, lost its *fundamental* institutional and symbolic value while very much remaining as a cultural and national *constant*. Everything happened as if Turks were *secondarily* Muslims. The cultural choices of the socio-political, economic and military elites between the years from 1920–1940 valued western life styles. Projects for religious reform, particularly in 1928, were clearly placing religion within the State's rationalist and nationalist challenges. However, the results of the political elite's exploitation of Islam were mixed. The speeches addressed to the people during the 1920's manifest a readily 'populist' approach to religion in that the intention is to strengthen the sense of being part of a determined and spiritualised national identity. However, during the 1930's and in the press of the search for a Turkish eternalism, certain theoreticians of the Kemalist revolution, sought to affirm the importance of the Shamanist and pagan roots of the Turks. These were used by the leadership as a resource for establishing a social and intellectual distinction from the people for whom these paganist cultural theories were not really accessible. The use of elements linked to paganism did in fact set the Turkish elite apart during the period of single party rule (that is pre-1946). It had no hesitation in encouraging the creation of national narratives to the point of lunacy, in making up myths of origin and of uniqueness (language, culture, ethnic origin, harking back to a lost superior civilisation from the continent Mu, all promoting Turkish supremacy etc.) These anti-Islamic reference points encouraged discrimination at the heart of Turkish society. This ideological construct and its complex relationship with Islam, albeit short lived, marked the subsequent, complex nationalism of the Turkish far right.

III The teaching of religion

The teaching of religious ritual was also subject to the dynamics of nationalisation. Ankara university's theology department, within which classical religious studies were treated on a historical basis,[8] the sole such department in Turkey in its time, closed in 1933. Nevertheless, the state continued to train Imams and maintained, albeit on a fairy tale and optional basis, a modest level of religious teaching in primary education. Between 1932 and 1950, a circular from the Ministry of Faiths (*Diyanet*), required the call to prayer in Turkish, and subsequent governments supported the translation of the Koran into Turkish, giving rise to both theologians and writers. The 'Turkisation' of rites and the access to the fundamentals of religion were specifically linked to a national policy of developing cultural uniformity.

The (re)opening of the theology department at Ankara university in 1949 can be explained in part by the transition to multi party politics in 1946, but also to the combined efforts of politicians, writers and intellectuals in justifying the importance of religion as a space for learning and culture. The roles of theologians could then be deployed: as actors in their university theology departments, as political actors at the heart of the Ministry of Faiths (*diyanet*), and more widely as symbolic touch points of religious representation. Theologians found themselves at the cross roads of a variety of fields. Called upon to train Imams and to build expertise in religious reforms, they produced informed advice on social phenomena and how they were mutating. According to the nature of successive governments their importance was either played down or increased, but since 1980 the number of theology departments in private Turkish universities has grown at an extraordinary rate.

This increase in the symbolic capital of theologians is a result, in part, of the earlier work of intellectual conservatives who, during the period 1940-1950, developed new spaces for religious thinking (the philosophy, psychology and sociology of religion).[9] At the same time, in so doing, they opened up the way for the rehabilitation of theology and a level of autonomy for it.[10]

The Turkish intellectual milieu also played a forward thinking role in bringing a new comprehensibility to Islam: that of a socio-political reference point. During the decade from 1930 to 1940, without opposition from the regime, new concepts were launched in university and cultural journals enabling the theorising and normalisation of religion's place in individual and collective contexts. Later, nationalism, liberalism, statism, and Islamism all manifested themselves with more or less levels of visibility. Conservative theories (*muhafazakâr*), proposed, to various degrees, ways by which the protection of national and cultural specificities might be assured, faced as they were with the dilution and desiccation of western modernity and sense of otherness. They developed religious themes in accordance with a political topology that denied exclusivity, were overtly critical of religious fanaticism and which recognised their quality as cultural glue and their capacity for mobilising the vital instincts of the individual and the organic state. Setting themselves as drivers and actors of the individual's liberal thinking, while opposed to an Islamic utopia, they built a complex dialectic. Their impact remains visible in Turkish politics to this day, where Islam has become a beacon for national identity.

The dilution of Islamic exclusivity in the republic's national priorities gave place to the promotion of a new morality (*ahlâk*). Religious in its origins, the notion was easily absorbed into the republican values and principles. It allowed the link between the republic and the national religion to be maintained. The teaching of religion in state schools was clearly based on the concept of morality, originally the discipline of religious sciences, just as the emphasis had been placed on spirituality in the university teaching of philosophy.

IV The link between religion and nationalism

The extreme right party presently active in Turkey, the MHP (Nationalist Action Party – *Milliyetçi Haraket Partisi*) set up in 1969, has played a major historic role in the link between religion and nationalism. A vast Turkish 'idealistic' (*ülkücü*) movement has been built by the bringing together, through a semantic and political construct, of areas of 'turko-islamic synthesis', with elements of anti-islamic symbolism – the symbol of the wolf, the origins of the Turks *gotürk*, etc. The recent history of the MHP, highly nationalist and populist, mobilising a fantasy of direct links between the people and the elite and the principle of popular direct action (through the example of private militias) can be characterised by a dual reference that is both Islamic and anti-Islamic. However, in recent times this party's lines seem to share a parentage with those of the AKP which, since the restart of the war with the PKK and the fall out from the attempted coup of 15 July, 2016 have monopolised the nationalist repertoire.

The arrival of the AKP in power in 2002 (Party for Justice and Development), partly originating from an Islamic party proscribed to allow for a take over of the state through a legislative approach (*Refah*, dissolved in 1998 by the Constitutional Court) can readily be interpreted, and partially rightly so, as a return to Islam in its populist form. The governance and policies of the party during its first term however caused astonishment: political pragmatism, the concerns of Europe, efforts towards the recognition of minority rights (Kurds, Alevis, Armenians). In so doing it presented itself as an incarnation of lay democracy within the context of a Muslim culture. But since 2013, preceded by some early warning signs, the trend has been reversed. The events in Gezi Park much covered by the media,[11] have shown an authoritarian power violently repressing demonstrators using political rhetoric to describe them as 'enemies of the nation'. The resumption, following various attacks, of hostilities with the PKK to the east of the country, sounded the death knell of any opening to the claims for autonomous political power for the Kurds. Despite all of this, which seemed from Europe to point to a break down of popular support for Recep Tayyip Erdogan, his party, the AKP, has regularly been re-elected to lead the country by comfortable margins. Manipulations of the media and the electoral processes are not sufficient to explain this repeated popular support, further strengthened by the attempted coup of July 2016.[12] Putting aside Erdogan's political charisma, the party leader who became President of the Republic, one of the major themes of the consolidation and continuing hold on power of the AKP lies in its political arguments. These set out a discourse around corrupt elites, habitually fleecing the people and around the AKP's capacity to address basic hopes and needs, ignored and mistrusted by former governments. In a range of elections, AKP candidates have regularly and massively claimed the concept of an approach to political operations called *Hizmet*. This signifies 'service' within a very broad approach incorporating charity.[13] A highly Islamic notion, this refers back to the electoral process as a means of the distribution of wealth and the promise of positions ahead of the elections, and also of municipal social actions. Wide spread social security and third party payments are sometimes accounted for as acts of the generosity and Islamic spirit of a one party government towards the people. Generally speaking, although something without precedent, the interests of the people (*halk*) are presented as being the alpha and omega of the AKP's political actions. This 'populism' leans on religion as a way of life and as social and collective glue. The rites and figures of Islam guarantee a thematic energy, a referential evidence base. The models of prophesy and charity are valued. The rituals of 'holy week',[15] the birth of the prophet are promoted and invested in by the State. Whilst favouring growth of the private economy, the AKP has established mixed areas (public/private) where it maintains a position of lavishing capital (through, for example, large scale public infrastructure works and real estate) so sustaining the corporate links that contributed to its election.

The success of the AKP doubtless lies in its capacity to have fulfilled the aim of the Turkish hard right party, the MHP – something it had never managed to do itself: *the bringing together of nationalism and religion*. These two components of the historical equation, and which led to the period of institutional instability and guerrilla action in the 1990's, were linked by the AKP in a way that was particularly adroit and apparent to those layers of society frequently absent from political discourse – unless through the classic litany of the representation of the people by the elite. If this has been and continues to be brutal for certain segments of society habitually held in esteem (cultural, university and military elites), the leadership of the AKP has highlighted in its propositions, if not in its political actions, areas hitherto little represented (conservative professional organisations, centres of commerce, the wearing of the veil etc.) The period of transition from the end of the 1990's to the arrival in power of the AKP at the beginning of the 21st century has allowed the updating of the deepest historical movements through a progressive resumption of collective activities, following the 1980 coup and other earlier efforts, in intellectual and economic fields by liberal conservatives.

V Conclusion

Our historical panorama has had the aim of shining a light on the coming together of populism and religion in present day Turkish politics. We have pointed to the dynamics of theology and religious representation that have been, and are occasionally, spaces of differentiation and struggle against the injunctions of the State. For conservative republicans, in particular, religion has been valued as a place of resistance against the closing down of politics and for individual freedom, fostering a vital energy and a spirit of spontaneity in people. Exploited for political ends, religion has been associated with populist nationalism to enable the aim of the standardisation of the country and its people to be realised. The Turkish example shows that the dialectic between religion and national identity is not a matter of course. It is a construct, where religion which offers a range of co-productions of political modernity, can be used either as a means of subversion or as a means of social and cultural standardisation. It is, depending on the circumstances and just like the theologians, an essential link; either of liberal thinking intruding on lay authority; or of a nationalism strongly coloured by morality and the demands of cultural and social structures and which prevents subversive divergence. It is therefore an instrument of social control. Religion is not however, *per se*, either an adjunct or an adversary of political regimes and their vacillations. It is what political practice makes of it. All the same, it is self-aware and finds its place, not through the external concepts applied to it but rather through the experience and practices of the faithful.

Translated by Christopher Lawrence

Notes

1. The Law of 1934 obliged each citizen to select a Turkish patronym to be passed to descendants
2. The Turkish word is *halkçilik*, drawn on the root *halk-*, people.
3. Based on Marcel Gauchet's modelling of developments in Christianity
4. Various proposals for a non lay regime have, for some years now, regularly been out forward by journalists or by member of the ruling party. These should be consider together with the valuing of a way of life placing religion, both ritually and symbolically at the centre of society.
5. Secularised in the sense that this does not imply primary actions by the State
6. Amongst the representatives and leading lights of this theory, men such as Ziya Gökalp, Yusuf Akçura, Ahmet Agaoglu, periodicals such as *Genç Kalemler* (Les jeunes plumes, 1908) and *Türk Yurdu* (La patrie turque, 1911), and an association, *Türk Ocagi* (Le foyer turc, 1912). Cf. François Georgeon, ' la montée du nationalsime turc dans l'État ottomn (19008-1914). Bilan et perspectives', *Revue de l'occident musulman et de la Méditerranée*, No 50, 1988. *Turquie, la croisée des chemins*, under the directionnof Daniel Panzac, p.30-44.

7. Opposed to the Sulktan, these reformers, re-established the constitutional monarchy of 1876 that he had abolished in 1878.
8. Dilek Sarmis, 'Conceptualiser le mysticisme dans une perspective académique: la constitution d'une histoire générale du mysticisme chez Mehmet Ali Ayni (1868-1945)', *European Journal of Turkish Studies* [Online], 25 | 2017, Online since 20 December 2017. http://journals.openedition.org/ejts/5451
9. Amongst them, some universities and human and social science departments that were strongly influenced by Bergsonian philosophy.
10. A return to prayer in Arabic, or more recently the authorisation of religious bodies, following an increasing visibility of provincial professional bodies.
11. The movement occupying Gezi Park (Istanbul) was started in June 2013 by local opposition to the AKP's policy of excessive urbanisation. This gave rise to protests on a significant scale that became a general challenge to the AKP regime.
12. An abortive attempt ascribed to the Fethullah Gülen movement, an enemy to Erdogan and leader of an international movement based in the United States
13. Ayse Buğra, 'Globalization, poverty, and the new politics of social policy: the case of the political economy of charity in Turkey,' IPSA World Congress, Santiago, Chili, July 2009.
14. Cf. Elise Massicard, 'L'islamisme turc à l'épreuve du pouvoir municipal. Production d'espaces, pratiques de gouvernement et gestion des sociétés locales,' *Critique internationale*, no. 42, Janvier-mars 2009, pp. 21-38.
15. *Kutlu doğum haftası*, considered by its detractors, largely inspired by Salafism or Quietism, as a reprehensible innovation -*bidat*- drawn from the Christian sacralisation of Jesus.

Part Two: Analyses

Religious Populism: the New Avatar of Political Crisis

FRANÇOIS MABILLE

Present day politics have been marked by an unforeseen return of religion to the public domain and the political arena. Since secularisation and progress appear to have distanced confessional protagonists as much as religious fantasists, we are now seeing new forms of linkages between politics and religion. Political parties referencing religious culture have emerged, within a context of an awakening nationalism. This article sets out to understand the reasons for the emergence, in a context marked by deep social inequalities, of a crisis of political representation and increasing doubt about the sovereign state.

One year after the fall of the Berlin Wall and the end of the soviet empire, Francis Fukuyama the political commentator, published his subsequently celebrated work, 'The end of history' (1992), in which he heralded the triumph of liberal democracy over all other political regimes. Twenty six years on, the same Fukuyama raised the, 'new tribalism and the crisis of democracy' in the American journal *Foreign Affairs*, picking up on the now common observations by political scientists of 'illiberal democracy', 'authoritarian democracy', 'authoritarianism', 'the return of nationalism', 'populism'. These are semantic variations that all reveal the present day log jams inherent in the model of classic liberal democracy and which are evidenced by successive and similar electoral outcomes: Trump's US election win, Brexit, the authoritarianism of the Turkish regime, the rise of the extreme right in Germany, Italy and France where the populists of left and right today make up the centre ground of political strength; we could also add examples from Hungary, Poland, Thailand... These different currents of populism re-articulate the range of political resources and symbols in both classical and hitherto unseen ways, including religious ones.

With a brief definition of the characteristics of populism, we can rapidly run through the different kinds of connectivity between populist politics and religion.

The history of populism is well known from its emergence in Russia and the United States at the end of the 19th century through to its full flowering in Latin America in the following century (examples being the Presidents of Argentina, Juan Peron and Brasil, Getúlio Vargas). The roots of this populism are easily discernible. They can be fully accounted for through the limitations of economic globalisation, the sense of a de-layering of social strata and the cultural uncertainty affecting the middle classes. Economic globalisation has indeed reduced levels of poverty, notably in lesser developed countries; however, in western democracies, the failure of policies for the redistribution of wealth and the pulling back of the Welfare State have hit the middle classes directly, while social dumping on a global scale, intensified by emergent new technologies that make the less skilled more fragile (thus jobs that are poorly qualified and paid), has marginalised the working classes.

Reformist politicians in social democratic parties (under their different guises), have become too scarce in political society. They are either too moderate or too complex in how they get across their political message to satisfy an electorate that lacks ways to interpret an international reality which, as symbolised in immigration, they find threatening. The consequence of this lack of capacity is directly seen in the return to a broken up, fragmented world: globalisation is being succeeded by a return to frontiers, and the building of real or symbolic walls (Mexican border, the 'take back control' slogan of the Brexiteers ranged around the anti EU UKIP party); the rebuilding of a 'one of us' approach that is both imaginary and fantastical in its supposed homogeneity. It is at this precise moment that populism makes its appearance: simplistic approaches, supported by myths of conspiracy or treachery, are taking the place of complex decryptions of the world.

The political scientist Jan-Werner Müller[1] analysed it well, stating that the populism set out its stall against two specific target areas:

aimed externally, in making itself the voice of a homogeneous people opposed to foreigners who do not look like them: the figure of the immigrant (along with all the conspiracy and take over theories), Muslim terrorism – Sunni or Shia (under various guises in Turkey, Iran and the US, a multicultural Europe (UK, Germany, Italy, France, Hungary, Poland), western Americans and Europeans (Russia), the financial oligarchs, and so on...

aimed internally, where the populist politician sets himself up, a classic rhetorical device, as the representative of the true people in opposition to the elite and to minorities as well (an example would be the Romany people in Hungary and Poland).

I The hijacking of the religious label by politics

The first articulation of populism with regard to religion has its roots in reactionary rhetoric, in the proper sense of the term, a rhetoric that exists in the political moment of resistance to change and of returning to a previous state that is either real or imaginary or, even more, of a resistance to cultural developments frequently presented as being linked to the minorities' rights. If the economic crisis places our material heritage at risk, the social and cultural crisis, according the political scientist Dominique Reynié,[2] extends this to placing at risk the '*non-physical heritage*', that arises from 'tradition', 'custom', be this architectural (mosques competing with churches) or people of faith (in their cultural identities). This is where globalisation has led to a crisis of identity: Reynié and Fukuyama are at one on this, the one evoking for example 'the identity sickness of the Europeans' with the other believing that: '*Politics today, however, is defined less by economic or ideological concerns than by questions of identity*'.[3] It is right wing populism that most easily seizes upon people of faith, viewed as vectors of tradition, as a means to restore an imaginary continuum, and also as possible cultural glue. Right wing authoritarianism, denying any possibility of debate, sits very easily with a religious culture that emphasises a figure of authority at its heart.

The populist right in present day Europe, as in the recent Trump campaign, knows how to hijack another element of religion.[4] Behind the distinction between the elite and the people, a moral distinction is also emerging which is, essentially, an exercise in moral impairment. There are both the people who are against the 'corrupt' elite and, of course, the additional need to identify the 'good' people, the people at large: this is the question posed not long ago by Trump, in his task of building opposition between those he took to be representing and the rest, ' Hands up if you are not a Christian conservative,' instructed the American leader. A distinction is created here using religion that takes us back to a supposed fundamental characteristic of the nation: a henceforth white protestant majority, a cultural homogeneity which preceded the fragmentation that arose from an assertion of the rights of minorities. We can see this in France in the Catholic vote, largely in favour of the right and extreme right, spurred on by a radical conservative movement, *Sens commun*.

Maurras' role in the inter- war years is being played out again in the links between present day populism and religion where total nationalism has set out to exploit religion, the latter expressing not a set of beliefs and far less spirituality but simply a sense of belonging, a marker of identity that is inseparable from that of the national community.

There can be no doubt that the European populists also highlight other characteristics. The case of Italy is interesting in understanding the workings of populism and its blockages: founded in 1989 by Umberto Bossi, La Liga is the result of the merger of the Lombardy Liga and ten regional movements from the north of Italy which were also advocate autonomy. Initially, the Liga Norte claimed the independence for Padanie, an imaginary region which corresponds to the Po valley. Here we see the north-south divide, but which is expressed not only in economic terms (rich north against poor south), but also in terms of ethnic oppression of colonialism and of autochthonism. The people from the south presented as 'shirkers', invaders living off the Padan people. The Liga's populist approach recycles a long familiar anti–southern stance, in categories of its own devising, and in the context of an end-game in the political cycle of traditional political parties struck by obsolescence.

Politically and culturally, the Liga presents a synthesis of populist programmes: xenophobia (2009: a 'white Christmas' launched by a mayor in the Liga to incense the foreigners in his area), racism (February 2018, an attack against six Africans by a former candidate from the Liga Norte), which was not condemned by Matteo Salvini, the denunciation of an 'immigrant invasion'; at a European level, the Liga presents itself as a champion of sovereigntists and eurosceptics wishing to leave the Eurozone, characterised as a German stitch up. Austria is another interesting example following the assumption of power by the Party for Austrian Liberty, (FPÖ). Islamophobia and xenophobia, weigh heavily at the heart of their programme as well as nationalist politics. Symbolically (but not uniquely!), the three sovereign portfolios that fall to the FPÖ are: Defence, Foreign Affairs and the Interior Ministry. The profile of the Austrian Chancellor is also worth noting: at the age if 31, the conservative Sebastian Kurz became, the youngest of world leaders, having taken the reins of the Christian Democratic party (ÖVP) just eight months earlier. This fills out a picture of a culturally attractive lay out of the extreme right by providing the idea of a continuity that is less disturbing than any openly attached to the roots of the extreme right party. In both cases one can see how populism uses religion both as a repellent (the perceived Islamisation of society) and as a marker of cultural resistance (Christianity as a basis of a common cultural identity). The Polish government, criticised by the Polish episcopate, has gone down the same path.

II Religion, fantasies and symbols

However, to see in the links between populism and religion only how the instrumental character of religion can be of profit to political entrepreneurs, would be to do an injustice to the complexities of the processes that are taking place. For, if globalisation has overturned the good ordering of liberal democracies and marked out traditional political parties for their relative weakness, it has also had an impact on religion. Globalisation has accelerated the mobility of religious beliefs, the creation of competing religious approaches through the framework of new communication technologies and the growth in diasporas; it also calls to them as producers of substitute fantasies, faced with the crisis in fantasy politics accelerated by the end of the East–West divide. Brazil is a good example of religious change, of the winning over by religion of those who have been excluded. On a foundation of social exclusion and rapid urban growth, the Catholic Church has presented itself as being at the centre and not at the margins. Having undergone an erosion of their liberation theologies, evangelists have developed a theology of prosperity aimed at thwarting the impact of liberal globalisation while promoting a thorough going moral conservatism which also sets out to oppose both the people's view that the elite are corrupt and their imagined views of the roots of internal corruption:

this leads, for example, to the rejection of the Afro-Brazilian religions, despite the their close ties to local cultures. Thus, the progression of ultra conservative evangelism has created the indispensable fertile ground for the emergence of Jair Bolsonaro: former soldier, reactivating the triptych of 'security, family, property', the populist leader who changes religion to get close to a religious movement which has the wind in its sails, who then presents himself for election to berate the corrupt elite, whip up insecurity, promote private Catholic education, and to denounce the 'gay tool-kits' distributed to primary schools.

This approach, using the outbreak of populism to create an opportunity for society to work upon itself, is one that is also characteristic of Masha Gessen's analysis in his book on contemporary Russia, *The Future is History*, showcased in an article by Michael Kimmage entitled significantly: *The People's Authoritarianism. How Russian Society Created Putin*. However, the title of Gessen's book also symbolises this reversal of perspective: cultural history has long been fertile ground for political enterprise. If Putin has enjoyed undeniable success, according to political scientists, it is through the work of reactionary philosophers such as Alexander Dugin:

> Inspired by Eurasianist thinkers such as the ethnographer Lev Gumilyov who trumpeted the 'essential nature of ethnic groups', Dugin forsees a unique destiny for the Russian people. For Dugin, a defining feature of Russia is its absolute separation from the West. He has argued for a martial foreign policy conducted along civilisational lines.[5]

Seen from this perspective, religion is in a considerable position, as the Ukrainian crisis has recently shown. Orthodoxy provides the cultural and imagined historical setting that allows a homogeneous coming together both against neighbouring Muslim countries and against a western Europe seen as decadent; in terms of foreign policy it also draws on *soft power* providing a vehicle for expansion and potential cultural influence.

Here we come to some important aspects of the relationship between religion and populism: the criticism of corrupt elites, the denunciation of liberal morality and the social consequences of ultra-liberal economics, accompanied by a re-reading of history and a perception of a duty to fight the country's decadence (and not just its decline). These sentiments are very strong in the United States and in Trump's rhetoric but also just as much for Putin or Turkey, vide Erdogan's speeches. Religion provides a rich source of symbols and historic legends that enable the manufacture of multifaceted enemies: the restoration of the Ottoman Empire against other Sunni states and, of course, Iran; the restoration of Russian grandeur based around its historic territories, with a cultural dimension of re-conquest which it brings us to its geopolitical demands: Ukraine, the cradle of orthodoxy, has as much value for the religious symbolism it represents as does the capture of territory it brings in strategic terms.

The notion of decadence, multifaceted and controversial amongst historians, is also helpful when it comes to analysing the case of France where, as with many others, it serves as a catalyst for the parties of the right and the extreme right.[6] The shift of political life to the right and the clear swing of the Catholic vote towards the conservative and extreme right (e.g. Front National Marine le Pen's Rassemblement National party), show in particular show how Catholic identities are also affected by economic and cultural globalisation. Patrick Buisson, an intellectual of the European extreme right, who sees himself in the tradition of Maurras and as a figurehead for the defence of the West, was the brains behind Sarkozy's ideological about-turn in his recent re-election attempt. Buisson inspired the Catholic movement '*Sens commun*' in its support of François Fillon, the conservative candidate of the right, during the recent French presidential elections, as he did the stance of the extreme right Marion Maréchal Le Pen: these days, Buisson has come out for 'Christian populism'. For him, culture is foremost: between sovereigntists and globalists there is a civilisational divide at play, producing what he describes as a demarcation between those for 'identity' and those for a 'diversity' that is in favour of multiculturalism. His denunciation of 'economism' is rooted in secular Catholic criticism of capitalism, 'a secular religion': his criticism of cosmopolitan globalisation is also very much due to a specific link to the tradition of territorial roots, where one readily finds the distinction between the legal and real concepts of country. From which comes support tagged to Viktor Orban, seen as a conservative, and also for '*La Manif pour tous*' (French movement against same sex marriage), which he stresses as 'a revolt against the economic horror of a consumer society with the objective of imposing the principle of '*illimitato*' (no limits), a true metaphysical driver of liberalism.' 'Essentially, he goes on, Orban's illiberal democracy, is very close to what I have called the era of Christian populism'.[7] In this, Buisson converges with the Catholic integralism represented in France by the *L'Homme Nouveau* periodical, which defends populism in saying:

> 'Populism' is a simple word to cover an array of phenomena whose common denominator is a visceral refusal to accept a fragmented liberalism approach. From whence the demands for security, national limits (rediscovery of the protection offered by national borders), for an authority that enables government by the people in ways consonant with their history and culture, etc. Populism can thus be understood as a resurgence of politics in the face of a triumphal and dehumanising economism.[8]

This resurgence of politics is a struggle against decadence seen in cosmopolitan terms (hence the denunciation of immigrants and xenophobia), against the end of frontiers that defined communities' physical contours (hence the pursuit of sovereignty and the denunciation of Europe), against the loss of values, Christian ones in this case, that bind communities together (hence the denunciation of Islam on the one hand and the rights granted to minorities on the other): complaints against homosexuals and marriage rights.

At a European level, we find all these more or less nuanced approaches at the heart of the Christian conservatives parties that have come together in the *European Christian Political Movement*. This movement has denounced everything that has come from cultural and economic liberalism and seeks to restore a value system that only the Church can provide. It is an approach that is fairly similar to those we find in right wing extremist and nationalist parties, none of whom hesitate to put religion on their constitutional political agendas, as we have been able to see with the right wing Justice party in Poland and Fidesz in Hungary.

III The equivocal nature of the figurehead

A final aspect remains to be considered, only too apparent and yet uncomfortable to analyse: in order to be successful, whether the forces of populists part company with politics to assure themselves of the resources offered by religion or whether they root themselves in a religious culture to seek a political opportunities, they will always have need of a political figurehead, a leader, a chief. Clearly, this not only specific to them, it is for any and every political party to choose its officers and leaders. However, the specific requirements for leader of a populist movement lead us, necessarily, to examine the various strands of populism itself, beyond what the overall programme might be. If we only define populism in relation to what it invents about exclusion, its xenophobic rhetoric, we would only succeed in grouping together right wing populists. Whereas in Latin America, the United States and also in Europe, left wing populism has flourished (Sanders, Mélenchon, Podemos etc.) A deeper consideration, following a Max Weber type approach to sociology based around charisma, would also lead to think about populist religious figures and their characteristics. In a certain way, Pope Francis is a good example of how populist traits can sit alongside a traditional figure of religious authority. His virulent criticism of the Curia, (the fifteen 'spiritual diseases'), his approach to seeking the support of public opinion against the elite, as represented by the cardinals, his recent condemnation of 'clericalism', his use of informal language including forceful phrases, all place him amongst them. His own cultural style of politics, redolent of Peronism,[9] and his 'people's theology'[10] make for a concept of leadership that is somewhat paradoxical: for the Pope is both at the same time a man of simplification in ways that are occasionally abusive and also the man who published *Laudato Si'*, his encyclical embodying complex intellectual thought in Catholic culture. His anti-liberal approach to economics brings him closer to populists of the left while his anti-liberal approach to morality shows common ground with those of the right. There is nothing surprising in this as the Pope fits well the role of Catholic social thinking icons faced with the present day challenges of liberalism in politics, culture and economics. And yet his singular example might allow us to highlight what it is specifically that makes for populism. In part, there is the challenge posed against the word of a measured leader and teacher, confronted by complex situations and the short-term dynamic of social media. In his desire for reform, the Pope finds himself, by the very nature of his role, facing the same challenges as all political leaders and so seeking the responses which these require: time management (the pontifical tenure is not long) making impossible any real reform of the approach to teaching, the difficulty of building consensus serving to bolster division and power differences. Furthermore, there is the long acknowledged difficulty[11] of maintaining one consistent narrative to a range of diverse audiences[12]: the present crisis also sits within the pontificate's claim to be a universal voice, in the face of plural Catholic identities confronted by hitherto unknown cultural and social challenges.

IV Conclusion

Religious populism therefore brings us leaders who are close to us, in spite of the wider context, and who draw upon the revival of nationalism. The way in which they use religion can be likened to an exploitation of religion as both a marker of identity and as a provider of a shared fantasy rooted in history, opposed head-on against the disruptive approaches of financial capitalism and present day progress, as typified by post-modern technologies. Their limitations, nevertheless, are contained in the roots of their success: religious populists are forces of opposition and protest that, to a certain extent, are competitive and cannot come together. Their national exclusivity prevents any attempt to build international structures; they can tear down international political systems but they cannot build new ones. It is their first stumbling block at a time when the challenges are increasingly global. The second lies within their difficulty in presenting a coherent approach to the differing approaches and challenges of liberalism. This latter point, it is to be remembered, concerns politics as much as the economy, and the public domain as much as the private. At a time of strong individualism, there is a second difficulty in this that is political and ideological in nature that the expression, 'illiberal democracy' perfectly symbolises.

Translated by Christopher Lawrence

Notes

1. J-W Müller, *Qu'est-ce que le populisme ? Définir enfin la menace*. Paris, Premier Parallèle, 2016.
2. D. Reynié, Populismes, *la pente fatale*, Paris, Plon, 2011.
3. F. Fukuyama, 'Against Identity Politics. The New Tribalism and the Crisis of Democracy', *Foreign Affairs*, sept.-oct. 2018, vol. 97, n°5, p. 91.
4. Cf. N. Marzouki, D. McDonnell et O. Roy (dir.), *Saving the People ? How Populists Hijack Religion*, London/New York, Hurst/Oxford University Press, 2016.
5. M. Kimmage, 'The People's Authoritarian. How Russian Society Created Putin', *Foreign Affairs*, jul.- aug. 2018, vol. 97, n°4, p. 181.
6. Very interesting take on the historical perspective in M. Winock, *Décadence, fin de*

siècle, Paris, Gallimard, 2017.
7. P. Buisson, *Le Figaro*, 15 juin 2018.
8. Thierry Colin, 7 mars 2017, https://www.hommenouveau.fr/1933/politique-societe/comment-apprehender-le-populisme--.htm
9. Cf. A. Livereigh. *The Great Reformer*, London, Picador, 2015.
10. Cf. R. Luciani. *Pope Francis and the Theology of the People*, New-York, Orbis Books, 2017.
11. Cf. M. Merle et C. de Montclos, *L'Eglise catholique dans les relations internationales*, Paris, Centurion, 1988. They raised these difficulties some thirty years ago.
12. The variations in the official pontifical positions on abortion and homosexuality are good examples of this.

Masculinist Populism and Toxic Christianity in the United States

SUSAN ABRAHAM

This essay explores scholarly literature on Donald Trump's populist rhetoric that has been extremely successful with white American Christians. I argue that Trump's rhetoric subtly deploys the anxieties of white Christians and their sense of loss of privilege and power to reassert traditional and idealized views of masculinity. White Christians ignore Trump's public behaviour as satire even as his behaviour secures political power within the United States for them. Trump, as I argue, provides white American Christians with a believable figure of muscular masculinity, leaving them to express a specific form of patriotic and muscular Christianity.

I Democracy Imperilled

In the United States, populist rhetoric highlights racial and gendered essentialist identities through a specific idea of Christianity, which imperils American democratic institutions. American Christianity, which is largely evangelical White and Protestant in orientation, exemplifies the ideals of 'muscular Christianity,' emphasizing a particular view of masculinity and femininity. Muscular Christianity is also associated with the rise of Eugenics and its belief in white American masculine superiority. In the shared cultural context of muscular Christianity, American Protestantism and American Catholicism are barely distinguishable because they agree on the superiority of whiteness, the superiority of men and traditional gender roles in family and society. This context, described as militant Christian Evangelical Masculinity, or, muscular Christianity, is the context for the rise of Donald Trump and his brand of right-wing populist politics in the United States.

In the months leading to the election, it seemed to many that Hillary Clinton, with her experience and her clout would trounce her opposition, the fantastical Donald Trump. The fact that he was elected (even as he lost the popular vote), and continues to bulldoze through with a culturally and politically narrow conservative agenda is remarkable. His populist message hits home, even though he is no member of the class identified with 'the people,' and had never been identified, until his candidacy, with a Republican or conservative political agenda. Wealthy white masculinity, as the embodiment of what it means to be an 'American' and 'Christian,' has successfully beaten back bodies of colour and bodies of women encroaching on their presumed turf. While it is not true to claim that Clinton's success would have automatically led to the inclusion and participation of bodies of colour, the fact that Trump has succeeded to gain so much ground for the Republicans deserves careful consideration by scholars of religion and theologians.

In an essay written shortly after the US Presidential election of 2016, Catholic theological ethicist, Fr. Kenneth R. Himes asserts that the US elections present a contemporary agenda for Catholic social ethics. In the early days following the election, many academic arguments identified white race anxiety and loss of economic mobility as the reason for electing Donald Trump to the Presidency. Himes provides one more reason: that anger was the motivating force behind the rise of 'populism, a word coined to describe the People's Party that emerged during the 1890s in defence of rural and urban workers in the grip of monopolies and financial institutions.'[1] While populism's ideological stance is flexible, depending on the context, its main feature highlights that politics is a moral fight to the finish between the 'good people' and the 'corrupt elites.' In the US context, the last electoral cycle yielded two kinds of populists demonstrating that the composition of 'the people' and 'the elites' is highly contended. Each side constructs the other in an 'us-and-them' relationship. Himes points out that Bernie Sanders represented one kind of populist whose rhetoric stressed class inequality. In contrast, Donald Trump's strategy emphasized race and religious victim-hood imposed on 'the people' by immigrants and non-citizens.

Himes points out that both Sanders and Trump appealed to the anger and anxiety about economic issues felt by their constituents. Economic anxieties and loss of cultural power intersect with the changing nature of work and employment. Work has changed from a guarantor of economic stability and job security to a condition marked by precarity. A whole new class of workers, called the 'precariat' now only have access to temporary or perma-temp (longer term contracts) or contracted employment. They have no access to the 'American Dream' which solidified in the post war period of the 1950s. Workers are facing extremely reduced job security and incomes even as social services including education and health care have steadily lost state funding. US populist rhetoric capitalizes on the felt condition of precariousness by identifying scapegoats and villains on the other side of each divide.

Another critical issue that Himes identifies in US populism is its deployment of overt racism and anxiety at the loss of cultural and political eminence. With particular reference to Arlie Hochschild's book *Strangers in Their Own Land*[2] published right before the elections, Himes asserts that

> There is anger, for sure, but also mourning, a sense of sadness and grief over a lost life. The people portrayed in the book feel the loss of a religious culture in a secular age, the loss of a white majority to diversity, the loss of a way of life to global economic forces and the loss of hope for attaining the American Dream. There is also a feeling of resentment toward elites who seem indifferent to the pain of the white working class and even scorn the group as racists, homophobes and nativists.[3]

Of course, the lack of access to the 'American Dream' has always been a reality for Black and Brown people in the United States. As a new reality for White people, it has now bred a particular sense of displacement and alienation due to the anticipation of the same upward economic mobility that their parents experienced in the 1950s and 1960s. Hence, while Black and Brown people in the US report relative improvement in their circumstances for the past 40 years, white people see erosions of their power, influence and economic security. Trump's highly successful strategy was and continues to be to join the sense of displacement to the economic despair felt by the whites as a particular form of racial and gender victimization. The strategy requires playing to the stereotypes about racial, immigrant, religious, gendered and sexual minorities and their presence in the nation's cultural and political life.

In contrast to Himes' analysis, Republican and conservative commentator Carson Holloway argues that 'Christianity does not bar one from supporting a Trumpian politics of Machiavellian populism.' Clearly recognizing that Trump is no 'saviour' of Christians, Holloway, nevertheless also welcomes the stratagem of dividing to conquer. Holloway, therefore, in contrast to Himes' social analysis, points to a single reason why Trump is so effective in mobilizing his party and his base: Trump appeals to American Christian self-interest. The will of 'the people' is paramount and 'the people' are those legal citizens invested in national identity and national security, equal to personal and psychological identity. Self-interest, self-governance and American supremacy are core aspects of North American right-wing populism, but it is also intimately tied to Christian religious identity. More importantly, Holloway makes a very important connection between Trump's Machiavellianism and his masculinity:

> In light of the outpouring of criticism from elites, it is more than a little ironic that Trump appears to have more integrity than many politicians. This stems, in part, from his forthright approach. He makes few appeals to noble principles, and thus there is little for him to betray. Moreover, he seems to remain true to his Machiavellian populism… Trump's preoccupation with manliness and strength is legendary. It is likely he thinks it would be weak and dishonourable for him to abandon positions he vigorously affirmed during his campaign.[5]

Holloway goes on to suggest that even though Trump's personal failings may bring pause to Christians, he is the best choice in the circumstances because, 'truly principled statesmen' though 'most desirable, are rarely available.' In other words, Trump is the best solution for Christian Americans at this time. Electing Trump and supporting his government is to take Scripture to heart, where Christians are enjoined to be 'wise as serpents and innocent as doves,' even as they acknowledge that Trump is a less than perfect candidate as President. Such rhetorical rationalizing is astonishing given the fact that the Christian conservatives in the United States generally have demonized candidates for the Presidency if their perceived religious identities and moral qualities are questionable in any way.

Striking in both of these analyses is the framing of the argument for or against Trump through a cultural and religious lens. Both Himes and Holloway are academics, the one teaching Theological Ethics, and the other Political Science. Both men are Christian; Himes is Catholic. The one concludes with a social analysis advocating understanding and empathy between differing groups, and the other with a rationalization of what it means to accept a leader who does not embody culturally acceptable moral and religious views. At the heart of both arguments are disagreements of who belongs in a democracy and the role of religion in a democracy. For Himes, all belong, especially, the minoritized sections of the nation's people (including also white people facing economic hardship) and it is incumbent on Christians to foster pathways to deeper understanding. For Holloway, White, Christian, wealthy, and masculine people (supported of course, by their White and Christian women) belong; democracy is a forum to articulate aggrieved claims of how belonging is compromised by the advance of 'others.' For them, White Christianity is under attack in the United States.

II Masculinist demagoguery

While scholarly literature generally asserts that populism has little to do with gender issues, it also asserts that populism, like other political realities is often associated with powerful men. For example, Cas Mudde and Cristóbal Rovira Kaltwasser argue that the relationship between populism and gender politics is dependent in great part on the ideology of nationalism in which it manifests itself.[6] Their comparative study focusing on Europe and South America is instructive. In the oppositional relationship between the people and the elites, 'gender' issues do not follow predictable lines; often, women are leaders of populist movements, like Marine Le Pen in France or Keiko Fujimori in Peru.[7] In Northern Europe, populists cast immigration as threatening European gender equality and advancement. In contrast, in South America, there is more ambivalence about gender issues because the main issue facing populists is economic inequality. The authors point out that in both cases, gender issues are secondary to nationalist politics.

The situation in North America is no different. 'Muscular Christianity' which advocates traditional gender roles for men and women drives nationalist discourse. For example, Kristin Du Mez in her essay 'Donald

Trump and Militant Evangelical Masculinity' argues that evangelical Christianity in the US has replaced the 'Jesus of the Gospels with an idol of *machismo*.'[8] Since democratic practices have eroded the preeminence of white Christian males, there is a conflated sense that Jesus and Christianity are losing cultural value as well. Mez points out that the militant Evangelical masculinist vote for Trump is in continuity with decades' old efforts to reinforce 'family values' as a core area of evangelical concern in American politics, with its emphasis on traditional gendered roles. Also extremely successful is Trump's subtle strategy of linking Christian and White *machismo* to the security of the nation, a form of demagoguery. Despite his personal transgressions of traditional marriage, the countless dalliances with multiple women, Trump's unfiltered speech and braggadocio appeals to militant males as a form of *machismo* that can secure the place of White men and the supremacy of America as the world's superpower. As Mez asserts, 'On the role of gender in the 2016 election, most observers have scrutinized Clinton's appeal or lack thereof. Still, more revealing is Trump's testosterone fuelled masculinity, which aligns remarkably well with that long championed by evangelicals. What makes a strong leader? A virile (white) man. And what of his vulgarity? Infidelity? Bombast? Even Sexual assault? Well, boys will be boys.' What Trump is modelling is that a man can have cultural power even in the face of the losses due to changing gender roles and the success of the women's movement, precisely by being an 'authentically' virile man (who abuses and debases most women as sexualized objects) but treats his (third) wife and daughters (somewhat) differently.

Populist demagoguery depends on convincing performances by a lead character. It is no surprise that Donald Trump is an expert at a particular kind of public performance. It all began with his reality TV show *The Apprentice*. His image in the show was the decisive 'CEO, business-man-in-charge.' The show made a clear connection between money and male power, a connection that Trump has successfully capitalized. He embodies the desire to secure power by being wealthy and his behaviour as a man actually secures the space for dominating male power in national politics. Even more effectively, Trump is channelling another nostalgic figure from America's TV past. In the 1970s, a highly popular sitcom on American TV called *All in the Family* depicted a man who was the opposite of 'politically correct.'[9] As entertainment, Archie Bunker provided both comic release and catharsis as tragedy. Bunker's overt racism, sexism and homophobia played on the anxieties of the 1970s: the instability of the postwar period and its sluggish growth, high oil prices, loss of manufacturing jobs and de-industrialization, together with foreign competition. He gave voice to White anger and fear of America as diverse. As satire, the show depicted Archie Bunker, and people such as he as relics from a bygone time. Yet, he also was a wistful figure—the 'Strict Father,' who called it like it is, evoking a homogeneously imagined cultural time and space.

For many, Donald Trump *is* Archie Bunker come to life, irreverent, funny, honest, and authentic, someone who nostalgically evokes the strict white Dad. Contrarily, they do not take Trump literally; now, schooled by Archie Bunker, they interpret Trump's behaviour as political satire against the hated liberal 'elites.' The people that voted for him understand the performative aspect of his words and actions. Yet, to take Trump seriously, as the people who voted for him do, is also to understand that the Archie Bunker phenomenon on television was the voice of 'the people,' though now, instead of a crude character on TV, he is the President of the United States. Trump is a better Archie Bunker than Archie Bunker! As a figure who occupies a very powerful position of power, Trump and his followers cannot be 'turned off' like a TV show. They are here, to occupy the centre of power because it rightfully belongs only to them. Hate speech, legitimized by the bully pulpit of the Presidency is effectively triggering multiple hate crimes around the US.

III Spectacular Masculinity

Right-wing Populism in the US is dependent on a media driven caricature of a lost ideal of white American patriotic masculinity. Its success depends on a central character craftily using a televised satire to play on the anxieties created by the loss of economic and cultural privilege. Trump's genius is that he creates and sustains a spectacle of patriotic masculinity that resonates with many American White men. Ethnographers Kira Hall, Donna M. Goldstein and Matthew Bruce Ingram in their essay 'The Hands of Donald Trump: Entertainment, Gesture, Spectacle'[10] suggest that Trump's use of the taboo through comedic gestures and behaviours offers a space outside of 'pure' religious and moral behaviours, effectively separating the sphere of the religious from political comedy. I think that this is a very interesting point that is undeveloped in their essay. Clearly, Trump is not a religious person. However, because of the performative significance of his behaviours, a space opens up for those who are religious to support him. Of scholarly interest here is the distinction made by historian Kevin Kruse between the separation of church and state, and religion in politics in the United States.[11] Trump is an ideal candidate; he represents the separation of church and state (and can be morally or religiously vacuous), while his followers represent the presence of politicized religion (and can enact their pious Christianity in service of the nation).

As ethnographers, the authors do not extensively dwell on the taboo breaking aspects of Trump's behaviour and do not explain how the separation of religion and religious belonging occur. Nonetheless, it is easy to understand that Trump's performance simultaneously crosses taboo barriers while inoculating spectators from the effects of that performance. For the authors, Trump's greatest success lies in his entertainment value. It is carnivalesque entertainment, different from reality. It effectively identifies Trump as the opposite of a 'religious' actor, as one who has the license, like a clown or a fool, to break rules with impunity. The arena of image, visuality and entertainment is easily the arena where outrageous and fantastic explorations of self and other, winning and domination take place, much like the American television entertainment of 'professional wrestling.' Trump, in fact, owns WWE (World Wrestling Entertainment) and has built his presidential persona around the organization's strongman methods. Additionally, Trump imports tactics employed in beauty pageants (he used to own Miss USA) to assert discordant standards of femininity for women. This allows him to make outrageous comments on women's bodies and looks, the way weak men assert their power over women. As the authors write, 'Beauty competitions do for femininity what wrestling competitions do for masculinity: they create a world of gestural performance based on an exaggerated and idealized notion of gender.'[12] Trump dominates by entertaining, and wins by bearing the taboo on behalf of his followers. He is the mythical hero, a colossus who saves his people through muscular masculinity.

Hence, while many white Christians like Carson Holloway above will acknowledge Trump's moral failings, the entertaining spectacle presented by his boorish public behaviour reinscribes idealized masculinity and idealized Christianity, all the while saving American Christians. Because of the separation of Church and State, it does not matter that Trump is a moral failure because his morality is irrelevant to politicized muscular Christianity. Simultaneously, because religion must animate the public sphere, his followers bring their moral, religious and masculine selves to their patriotism, unsullied by the taboo-crossing hero. It is the reason why White Christians take Trump's behaviour seriously. Because the locus of morality and religion is situated in the individual, the Presidential performance of crude humour and vulgarity exempts his followers from any personal culpability. Moreover, his crass behaviour and humour are directed at the enemies of 'ordinary Americans,' the people. The people, ordinary Americans, now take up the gauntlet of keeping America Christian and White. To take Trump seriously is to instrumentalize his performance for political gain whilst keeping a particular idea of religion and muscular Christianity in play.

Through the form of spectacle, Trump and his empire bring together 'many of the elements analysed by scholars as spectacle in late capitalism: hyperbole, casino capitalism, branding, simulacra, nostalgia, mediatization, excess, consumption, and vacuousness.'[13] Trump's use of spectacle in politics affirms the sense that politics is mostly about spectacle and show. Yet, because he does it in a particular way, to call out the 'elites,' he is also perceived as more trustworthy and reliable, a paragon of male power. The authors wonder why the privileging of style over content in Trump's spectacular performances 'win' despite the lack of substance and many political gaffes. In my reading, there are two reasons for this. The first, already alluded to, has to do with the notion that religion is after all a privatized and individualized experience, and Trump's taboo crossing proclivities protect White American Christians from culpability. Second, for those who support Trump ardently, there is the affirmation of personal and masculine individualism, since he presents the spectacle of the lone autonomous hero who resists any script for acceptable masculinity. As spectacle and taboo-crosser, he represents *the* form of successful and mythical masculinity.

In recent analyses of Trump's supporters in the US, scholars have named as 'toxic Christianity,'[14] the form of Christianity that understands masculinity in specifically White Christian terms. Trump himself is hardly Christian, but he resonates with Christian groups in America by reproducing an identifiable rhetoric of masculinity and Christianity, both of which are toxic. The context of such masculinity and religious identity is one of aggrieved identity politics. Jerry Falwell Jr., President of the conservative Liberty University, is quite content with the fact that Mr. Trump is less than an ideal Christian. When the 'grab them by the pussy' tape leaked, Falwell said, 'We're never going to have a perfect candidate unless Jesus Christ is on the ballot.'[15] Of course, such a rationalized opinion would not be forthcoming if the candidate represented the opposing party, as was clear with the many aspersions cast on Barack Obama's Christian and American identity by Trump and the Republicans. The win-at-any-cost of contemporary American politics thus blends a particular form of masculine identity to a particular form of Christian identity. It is a highly successful, if contextual, strategy for American right wing, conservative, Republican populism. Its Christianity is barely recognizable as the form of discipleship to Jesus. It is toxic because all it seeks is its own power, eminence and dominance.

A key feature of the elections of 2016 was the numbers of White women voting for Donald Trump. Right wing populism is often identified with angry white, nationalistic men. Scholars have been pouring over data attempting to analyse why so many white Christian women voted for Trump. One reason is that they are attempting to find economic stability for themselves, their children and their families. They are also angry that many public services go towards immigrants and refugees. Many women who voted for Trump are among the white underclass, dismayed and frightened by the impossibility of anticipated upward mobility. Voting in line with their men to guarantee their own economic stability is common, more so also because in many such communities, women are still dependent on men economically. Some commentators are wondering whether the induction of Justice Kavanaugh to the Supreme Court, given the mass of evidence against him of sexual violence, will lead to a women-led overturning of Republican power in the midterm elections. Nevertheless, the dismissal of the #MeToo movement by many conservative women gives lie to that wish. In a recent *New York Times* analysis, Republican women voting for Trump also reveal their deep anxieties about national security.[16] They are convinced that their world, white, Christian and conservative, is being destroyed internally and externally. When asked how they can support Trump's misogynistic behaviour, they scoff at liberal sensitivities. They see Trump as a hero and his behaviours as benign and non-threatening. One wonders at the extent of institutionalized sexism and nostalgic acceptance of *machismo* by these women, pitting gender against race in such a way that race difference trumps gender difference for white women.

IV Restoring Democracy

Gender, Race, Class, Religious identity and Citizenship are neuralgic and mutually contending issues in all democratic societies. These are also urgent issues for religious traditions, communities and scholars who must provide constructive religious and theological responses to the erosion of democratic processes by populist rhetoric. The challenge is to restore democratic institutions without propagating toxic and masculinist Christianity. This essay has identified certain critical pathways. As Ken Himes' essay argued, understanding and empathy between different groups is essential. Can we find Christian leaders who will be able to shape and form their communities to be more understanding and empathic by redefining the space of the nation as a shared space for women and men, the rich and poor? Instead of global economic and cultural dominance, can US Christians model a coequal responsibility for the flow of labour, finances and resources? And can such a sharing of responsibility lead to a redefinition of national security? These are tantalizing questions for a constructive non-toxic Christianity.

In the US, the Catholic Church has lost its credibility in the wake of the child abuse revelations. Its culture of secrecy and self-serving power has been shamefully revealed. Yet, US Catholic leadership and many of its conservative adherents pretend that the only issues of note are the advance of secularism and women's reproductive rights. If the American Catholic Church could model self-renouncing power by its all-male leadership and call for corporate repentance and public examination of its masculinist structures, it may yet be a Church for the times. If it can draw on its vibrant strand of liberation theology and option for the poor, there is hope that it might neutralize the reach of right wing racism to cultivate understanding and empathy for economically and politically disadvantaged citizens. Catholic theology has also consistently used capacious theological idioms like 'the people of God,' to redefine belonging in larger than institutional terms. Such inclusive idioms can help redefine democratic inclusion. If it can re-envision models of governance that keep men and male clergy in continuous power, albeit as benign and mild leaders, Catholic constructive theology may catalyse the creation of non-toxic communities. If it can embrace the role of religion in politics and call out the greedy, self-interested, self-serving fragile anxiety of White Christians, it will honour its prophetic calling. If not, it is a form of toxic Christianity, complicit and as responsible for the rise of exclusionary nativist and populist politics around the world as the worst populist demagogue currently in power.

Notes

1. K.R. Himes, 'The State of our Union' in *Theological Studies*, Vol 78(1), 2017, p. 148.
2. A.R. Hochschild, *Strangers in Their Own Land* (New York: New Press, 2016).
3. Himes, p. 158.
4. C. Holloway, 'Donald Trump, Principe' in *Opinions, First Things*, (August/September 2017), p. 12.
5. Ibid., p. 13.
6. C. Mudde and C.R. Kaltwasser, 'Vox Populi or Vox Masculini? Populism and Gender in Northern Europe and South America,' *Patterns of Prejudice,* Vol 49, 2015, p. 16-36.
7. Ibid., p. 21.
8. See https://religionandpolitics.org/2017/01/17/donald-trump-and-militant-evangelical-masculinity
9. See N. Scheper-Hughes, 'Another Country? Racial Hatred in the Time of Trump: A Time for Historical Reckoning', *Hau: Journal of Ethnographic Theory*, 7 (1), 2017, p. 449-460.
10. K. Hall, D.M. Goldstein, M.B. Ingram, 'The Hands of Donald Trump: Entertainment, Gesture, Spectacle,' *Hau: Journal of Ethnographic Theory*, 6 (2), 2016, p. 71-100.
11. K. Kruse, *One Nation under God: How Corporate America invented Christian America* (New York: Basic Books), 2015.
12. Hall & alii, ibid., p. 81.
13. Ibid., p. 91.
14. See https://www.theguardian.com/us-news/2018/oct/21/evangelical-christians-trump-liberty-university-jerry-falwell
15. https://www.theguardian.com/us-news/2018/oct/21/evangelical-christians-trump-liberty-university-jerry-falwell
16. See https://www.nytimes.com/2018/11/03/us/politics/trump-women.html?action=click&module=Top%20Stories&pgtype=Homepage

Part Three: Challenging Populism by Theology

The 'People of God' and its Idols in the 'One and Other' Testaments: How Sacred Scripture Challenges Populist Rhetoric

MARIDA NICOLACI

If, from the historiographical point of view, populism can be considered a modern phenomenon, the 'tribal' character of the conception of people which it underpins enables a consideration of the populist rhetoric in the light of the biblical message and an approach to the populist way of understanding, recounting and living identity in post-democractic societies in a 'religious' and, above all, prophetic manner of representing and understanding the dynamics of the construction of identity on the part of the 'people of God' which is spoken of in the Scriptures. The unexhausted fight against the fetishes set to protect an identity of a people monolitically conceived, disrespectful of otherness and intolerant of difference and plurality, in fact characterises the prophetic re-reading of the process of identity construction of the people of God in the One and the Other Testament and traces a path in which it is possible to integrate oneself to think, recount and realise a fraternal and inclusive construction of human society, truly productive for individuals and for communities.

'You're popular when you recognise yourself in the people, when you belong to them, you are populist when you build an idol in which the people can see themselves'[1]

To examine Scripture in the search for arguments which challenge populist rhetoric raises numerous terminological, methodological and hermeneutical problems, starting with the definition of the 'essentially contested concept' of 'populism'.[2] What are we referring to when we speak about populist rhetoric? How, with methodological rigour, do we bring biblical motives and models, culturally codified according to forms, contexts and political structures of pre-modern societies, to those in use in Western post-modern society and, even more specifically, in the American and European contexts where the growing assertion of so-called 'populist' governments and leaders seems proof of a crisis of representative democracy? The search in Scripture for input useful for a critical evaluation of populist rhetoric may be unjustified and anachronistic. Which Scripture should we turn to, then, and how should we avoid exploiting it to legitimise or delegitimise contemporary political models and strategies?

I will start, therefore, by stating what I mean here by populism. I will not be referring, as in historiography, to the different forms in which 'classical' political populism has gradually manifested itself in Europe and in America in the last 150 years, in close, if not exclusive, correlation with the assertion of democratic regimes.[3] Instead, in more structural terms I will refer to that 'varied kaleidoscope'[4] of doctrines, practices and political discourses – sometimes realised in a 'folkloric' and scientifically incorrect style – united by the representation of an identity (and desire) of 'people' based on an abstract and mythologised idea of that people, on the recognition of its members, on the consequent ostracism of those considered extraneous or dangerous to it, on the creation of fetishes capable of nourishing, strengthening and defending an identity which is monolithically conceived and immune, through specular rhetoric, to distinctions and complexity. Although often associated with a vertical contrast between 'people' and 'élite', the populist discourse to which I intend to refer is not just that which finds its specific nature in criticism of the establishment but that which, precisely as a *mood* or 'state of soul',[5] as an expression of discomfort and popular protest, is distinguished by its character which is in certain senses 'tribal' and therefore, paradoxically, pre-modern.

The liberal-democratic conceptions (and their historical derivations) stem in principle from the overcoming of tribal life. To shut oneself away in the presumed (fideistic) simplicity of intuition, to reduce the complexity of phenomena to some imaginary unique and elementary cause, to entrust oneself to a charismatic Leader and thus free oneself from the difficulty of having to understand the world on your own, are attitudes which conflict with the use of complex conceptual tools and generally amount to a regression to the pre-modern. Populism is regressing to an absolutised concept of people, aprioristic and, above all, idealised. The people are conceived indifferently as either the source of every good or of every evil (in the latter case it is 'common people'). It is nevertheless an indifferentiated entity... According to the particular ideological-political constellations, the presumed identity of a people rests either in 'religions', or in 'language', or in 'tradition' and 'culture', or in 'territory' where the people has settled, or in the antiquity and purity of its 'race' and 'ethnicity'.[6]

Pre-modern, therefore, can be considered The alliance between the connection between popular claims and the ostentatious attitude of the 'populist' leaders to the extolling of an abstract desire of the 'people' above and against any institutional mediation can therefore be considered pre-modern. Likewise the creation, subject to such an alliance, of a self-styled direct link between the leaders and 'the people' aimed at divesting the élites responsible for every form of corruption of authority seems too to be pre-modern. In the final analysis, pre-modern can be considered the 'basic morphological element' common to all the variations of the populist 'labyrinth', in other words 'the conviction that the real instrument for tackling and resolving the problems of the universe is fideism', be it expressed by the 'desire of a one truth of faith (not necessarily religious) rather than the use of differentiated truths in the plural',[7] with the obsessive need for a charismatic leader or, above all, of varied fetishes to set as a guard over one's own salvific fence (from time to time territory, religion, language, tradition, culture, race etc.).[8]

If, therefore, from the historiographical point of view, 'populism' correctly named is a modern phenomenon, what, in my view, enables the evaluation of the populist rhetoric in the light of the biblical message is the 'tribal' character of its construct. Perhaps unexpectedly, this permits us to approach the 'populist' way of conceiving, recounting and living identity (and political representation) in 'post-democratic' societies in the 'religious' and, above all, prophetic way of representing and understanding the dynamics of the construction of the identity of the 'people of God' of which the Scriptures speak.

The final necessary clarification concerns the scriptural point of reference within which the research is undertaken: I will examine the Catholic biblical canon in such a way, however, that the Christological re-reading and re-writing of the Scriptures of Israel (the New Testament as book) does not mean the rejection of their full autonomy (become the Old Testament of the Christian Bible). In the wake of the systematic intuition of P. Beauchamp, I will therefore refer to the 'One and Other Testament', the New intrinsic in the First (cf. Jer 31:31-34) not through chronological or theological continuity but through theological continuity.[9]

I The 'people of God' in the perspective of peoples

If, as the majority of exegetes opine, the redaction of the final form of Moses' *Torah* (Gen 1-Deut 34) did not see the light of day before the post-exilic reconstruction (VI-V century B.C.), and represents the interests and identity aims of the Jewish communities returning from Babylonian exile and gathering around worship, the Temple, and the Law, this is subject to the need for a people to recount its story in an effective and significant, salvific way, after repeated and evermore dramatic experiences of suffering in the relationship with neighbouring peoples and their superior political and military power, represented first by the Neo-Assyrian Empire and then by the Babylonian Empire. The restoration and safeguarding of the identity of Israel, in this stage more than in any other previous stage in its history, needs the pressing affirmation of the religious unity of a people which can no longer rely – or in any case not in an exclusive manner – on territoriality or political independence but only on something which precedes and, eventually, is based on both, in other words the relation of the constituent covenant with the one God (YHWH) from whom Israel derives its own distinctive unity and uniqueness in the midst of other peoples. The possibility of speaking about its own social and political identity now depends essentially on the preceding and foundational affirmation of its own originating religious unity/uniqueness. The account of the exodus from the land of slavery of the tribes of Israel, whose origins go back symbolically to the eponymous forefather Jacob-Israel (Gen 32:29) therefore becomes the foundational representative myth of the ethnic-religious identity of the people and the foundational motive –

then recited countless times, from the book of Exodus to that of Wisdom (cf. Wis 10:15-19:9) – of the inexhaustible hope of a threatened and often oppressed people.

At the same time, however, the myth of a common origin in time and space, 'essential for the constitution-construction of an ethnic commonality',[10] in the Genesis account which opens the Scriptures does not end with the patriarchs and the history of the people born from them, but extends powerfully to the point of including the common origins of humanity in male-female Adam (Gen 1:26-28), a way of saying that the unity which makes the human image of God – unlike that of animals, complex in its different species – is a task for the human person to be performed by living out fraternity and exercising a sovereignty which, in the divine plan, does not include violence and the shedding of blood (cf. the gift of just plant food in Gen 1:29-30). Read against the post-exilic backdrop referred to previously, the cultural and political impact of the choice to begin the self-narration not from the history/genealogy (the *tôledhōth*) of the progenitor Abraham from his father Teraḥ (11:27), but from the *tôledhōth* of the peoples of the sons of Noah (10:1,32), rooted in turn in the *tôledhōth* of Adam (5:1) against the backdrop of the *tôledhōth* of the cosmos (2:4). Right from the start of Scripture, then, 'there is just one subject which fills the whole of sacred history: the relationships of a people with all the peoples'.[11] This narrative choice manifests a constant of processes of construction of identity at the socio-anthropological level: 'an identity constructed as representative of a collectivity brings into play...a dialectic process of self-affirmation and exclusion, therefore 'we are us' precisely because 'we are not them'. To be, to continue to be 'us', it is necessary to call in others (neighbours or enemies)'.[12] On the religious level, then, it means 'the consciousness of a presence of the non-Jew in the Jew',[13] which runs through the whole of the biblical narrative from Genesis to Revelation, where the 'people of God' of the heavenly Jerusalem are spoken of irrevocably in the plural: 'And I heard a loud voice from the throne saying, 'See, the home of God is among mortals. He will dwell with them; they will be *his peoples*, and God himself will be with them" (Rev 21:3).

Therefore, as a foundational identity of the people of God, in the Torah which guarantees it and guards it in life, is the affirmation of a difference and original uniqueness which itself rests on the original unity of humanity in the difference of the many peoples which comprise it: how will the chosen people know and live its own uniqueness and difference? The Genesis myth of the origins seems to respond that the 'election is conceived as a difference by which the chosen one faces the universe. And it knows it'. For the 'people of God' of the Scriptures, the recognition and salvific respect of otherness, which simultaneously means the renunciation of any form of totalitarian claim, belongs 'genetically' to the awareness of its own election or particularity.

As confirmation of that, from a narrative point of view, the choice itself of Israel, inscribed in the *toledōt* of Shem (Gen 11:10) and in the history of the call of Abraham (Gen 12:1-3), seems to be the divine response to the idolatrous and totalitarian temptation of humanity represented mythically by the powerful account of the construction of *Babel* or Babylon (Gen 11:1-9). If, in fact, in 10:5,20,31,32 the diversity of languages, of families, of territories and of nations seems a well-founded given for the descendants of Noah and demonstrates that the differentiated plurality of peoples does not compromise but rather exalts the original unity and fertility of human beings, nevertheless in Gen 11 the town which the children of Adam (the *benē ādhām*)) want to build is based on the reduction of 'everything' to a repetitive uniformity: 'the whole of the earth' has 'one' language and the 'same' words (11:1) and the builders of Babel – already a place representative of the warlike and violent dominion of the king Nimrod and 'cradle of the oppressive empires'[15] (10:8-12) – want a city which represents its name (11:4), in other words the powerful and victorious identity, realising it as 'society without otherness' with building bricks all equal and in order;[16] they want the tower, architectural symbol of their triumph, to be capable of penetrating the skies, that is, to challenge the divine otherness, of reducing it to itself and taming it as sacred legitimisation of its own social and political plan. The only reason for this, then, is fear: 'Come, let us build ourselves a city, and a tower with its top in the heavens, and let us make a name for ourselves; *otherwise* we shall be scattered abroad upon the face of the whole earth' (11:4). The fear of geographic dispersal and difference which in the divine plan is rather the full sign of the blessing and fertility of humanity, drives the builders of Babel to the realisation of a totalitarian city whose members are all equal, whose communicative actions are mere repetition of a unique discourse and which, to succeed, is expressed through warrior leaders and hunters like Nimrod.

> The Babylon project is totalitarianism. It seems to have two driving forces: on the one hand the complicity of a people with its own slavery, a complicity moved by the fear of dispersal and by the weakness which would arise from this division and by confrontation with the stranger... On the other hand, the opportunism of a prince which makes the most of the desires and agonies of the people to make its name and strengthen its own power. It therefore seals with the seal of its own desire the popular thirst for a reassuring union and imposes on everyone the 'one thought' which they ask be guaranteed. Thus, unity is achieved as uniformity and aims at levelling out differences, wiping out the distinctiveness of individuals and groups, and eliminating real and potential discord. But what the account suggests with great clarity is that totalitarianism arises on the basis of a convergence of interests: fear of freedom and difference, on the one hand (11:4), thirst for power, on the other (10:8-10).[17]

Besides, there is nothing strange in this plan if the protagonist is a human being accustomed by serpentine language to the fear of what is lacking in everything and the consequent logic of jealousy and usurpation (cf. Gen 3:1-5). However, just as a life perpetuated in the denial of divine otherness and in the obsessive dominion of totality (cf. Gen 2:16-17; 3:4-5:22) would be death for human beings, so the building of a violent city based on the fear of plurality and difference (Gen 11:6-7) would be an uncontrollable curse. The divine reaction to both plans, therefore, is specular (cf. the parallelism between Gen 3:22-24 and 11:6-9).

Gen 11:6 is the first verse of the Jewish Bible in which the term '*am*, 'people', appears, the same term which in the rest of the Scriptures often designates Israel as people of YHWH, not uncommonly in contrast with every other nation (*gōy*) distinct by race, governance, language, divinity and territory. So the first time 'people' (*'am*) is mentioned, its monolithic connotation ('one people with one language') is presented as a danger for human coexistence. The chosen people will have to avert it above all in itself: 'Babel has revealed that humanity, in its cultural and political form, is sick. The election is understood as a cure. But this cure is homoeopathic, once again, marrying the form of the sickness. Are not the individual and everyone perhaps placed in violent opposition?'[18] Will not the chosen one be tempted to make of that choice a reason for the rejection of what is different or, even more dramatically, of the diversity within themselves?

II The people of God, its guides and its idols

The attraction of other nations' customs and divinities, periodically experienced in the course of the centuries-old history of Israel as more powerful, sometimes leads to an emphasis of the need for a marked contrast from strangers (cf. Ex 23:31-33; Lev 18:1-5.26-30; Deut 12:29-31; 20:16-18), symbolically and ritually expressed, for example, by the command of the *ḥerem* ('slaughter') in the context of the holy war (cf. Deut 7:1-2; 20:16-18; Josh 6-12; 1 Sam 15). As a whole, however, the open and laborious process of social construction in the structural recognition of otherness – of YHWH, of the neighbour and of the stranger within and beyond one's own boundaries – remains in Scripture the greatest identity challenge of the 'people of God'. It is no surprise, in fact, that a significant part of biblical legislation and its interpretation (cf. Ex 23:9; Deut 26:5-6) is devoted to relations with the stranger, especially the guest living within the territorial boundaries of Israel as a resident emigrant. The condition of displacement, distress and tension towards a better future for the emigrants ends up, in fact, expressing paradigmatically the existential condition of the human person and the holy people: 'we are aliens and transients before you, as were all our ancestors' (1 Chr 29:15; but cf. also Lev 25:23,35,47; Ps 39:13; 119:19; Heb 11:13; 1 Pet 1:1,17; 2:11). So, therefore, the Israelite must not 'oppress' and maltreat strangers (Ex 22:20; 23:9; Lev 19:33; Jer 7;6; 22:3; Ezek 22:7,29; Zech 7:10; Mal 3:5) but welcome them and respect their rights, in obedience to the command and in imitation of the One who, just as He was the support and defence of the patriarchs in their condition as emigrants, is the support and defence of the stranger (cf. Ex 22:20; Deut 24:14-18).

The process of the social construction of the people of God, in respect of each difference, remains the most difficult concern for its charismatic leaders to manage. The Exodus epic, which is its foundational myth, recounts it in terms of a battle for liberation from slavery. For the purposes of our reflection, at least two significant ideas can be gleaned from it. First the struggle for liberation, which is a struggle for the affirmation of its right to exist and to be other and different. This bears the risk of a difficult working out of life, not immune from nostalgic memories of the condition of slaves (deadly, but risk free) and, even, of the perverse bond of mutual attraction between master and slave. Consequently, whoever acts as spokesman and leader must be able to maintain the vital movement of differentiation up to its final outcome. That is what Moses must do, for example, in the face of the legitimate accusation of the scribes of Israelites (cf. Ex 5:21) or of the people in the desert (Ex 17:3), when he is at risk of lynching (cf. Ex 17:4).

Yet the battle for liberation reveals higher stakes when it manifests itself as a radical anti-idolatrous and essential challenge, the demand made of responsible human beings, the only permissible 'image of God' (Ex 20:2-5, 22-23). The magnificent account of the building of the golden calf (Ex 32; Deut 9:8-21; Neh 9:18-19; Ps 106:19-23), 'canonical place of idolatry' in the Scriptures,[19] paradigmatically represents the drama of difference and otherness at the very heart of the people of God. The liberating God and the prophets whom he sends as guides for his people in fact 'know' suffering (cf. Ex 3:7; 4:31; 5:22-23) but are not in absolute harmony with the people; the people, impatient of suffering and insecurity, are unable to manage otherness and are always tempted to 'appoint a leader to return to their slavery in Egypt' (Neh 9:17). During the forty days when Moses climbs the mountain to receive the Law of the covenant (Ex 24:12-18), in place of the liberating God, present in the cloud which covers the mountain (Ex 24:15-18), is placed a representation of the idol of gold, the young calf which makes the power and vitality which reassure the people tangible to the senses; in place of his prophet, who has lost control (32:1, 23), is placed someone who is responsible for giving to the idol the reassuring worship which the people needs. An identity fetish in answer to the fear of the unknown and the unwillingness of its own origin and its own future, the golden idol is therefore burned and smashed by Moses and the people who rushed to build it with their own valuables (Ex 32:20) are made to drink its ashes.

In a completely different era, in the monarchic period of Israel's history, it was above all the prophets – and not the 'court prophets' (cf. 1 Kings 22; Jer 28-29; Ezek 13) – who supported the people in their historical process of identification and difference fighting against the people and their leaders at risk of their own safety (cf. Amos 7:10-17; Jer 19-20; 26:20-23; 37-38). The anti-idolatrous battle remained their liberating mission par excellence: not only the battle against idolatrous worship in the proper sense but, with the historico-religious, political and institutional development of Israel, the battle, too, realised by the unmasking and denunciation of the chameleon forms which idolatry assumed even in the very worship of YHWH (cf. Isa 1:10-15; 29:13-14; Jer 7), in the traditions of the covenant and the theologumena of Israel as 'people of God': 'Surely the Lord is with us! No harm shall come upon us' (Mic 3:11). It is their task to point the finger at the leader and institutions who invoke the most sacred traditions of faith, which had become fetishes, as deceptive protection of the people nourishing a perverse mechanism of continual strengthening between social and ideological experience, the very thing which led the leaders to proclaim 'visions of peace' (*shalōm*), well-being, fullness and solidity where 'there is no peace' (cf. Jer 6:14; 8:11; 14:13-16; 23:16-17; Ezek 13:10,16) and where, rather, a violent and transverse injustice has profoundly sickened the social and political fabric of the people. Their arduous and dramatic mission is that of reporting the devastating effects which the hidden fetishes have in politics, in the economy, in the administration of justice and, even, in the interpretation of the Law, the 'last refuge of the idol'[20]:

> 'How can you say, 'We are wise, and the law of the Lord (*tōrath* YHWH) is with us', when, in fact, the false pen of the scribes has made it into a lie?' (Jer 8:8).

The definitive criterion which enables the unmasking of the idol for the prophets always remains the effective restoration of the practice of social justice ordered by the Torah and, particularly, the defence of the right of the weak, represented by the most exposed categories: the stranger, the orphan and the widow (cf. Ex 22:20-21; Deut 10:16-19; 14:29; 24:17-22; 27:19). What truly comes from YHWH is 'useful', beneficial, because it really is effective for the life of the people and the authentic safekeeping of the weakest which is its litmus test (cf. Isa 1:17.23; Jer 7:5-7; 22,2-4; Ezek 22:6-7; Zech 7:8-10; Mal 3:5); that of the idol, on the other hand, is the inconclusiveness and inability to save (cf. 1 Sam 12:21; Wis 13:16; Isa 44:9-10; 46:2; 57:12-13; Jer 2:8,11-13; 16:19; Hab 2:18). The fruitful practice of justice becomes the prophetic yardstick of the safekeeping of identity and existence itself: if the truth of the Law is betrayed and justice distorted, there is a return to the chaos preceding the creative act (cf. Jer 4:22-26).

III 'We had hoped that he was the one to redeem Israel...' (Lk 24:21)

The gospel *kerygma*, in the various forms which its literary testimony has assumed in the writings which then formed the 'New Testament' as a book, could be seen as the oldest testimony of the process of theological, ritual and social reconfiguration of that part of Israel which had recognised in the Galilean prophet and teacher Jesus of Nazareth the Messiah expected for the end time of its own liberation (the Christ), drawing from that extremely significant consequences for its own identity as 'people of God', right up to considering it – as eminently represented by the Pauline mission and reflection – as now inclusive of pagans independently from their incorporation into Israel 'according to the flesh'. From a hermeneutical point of view, I think this process can also be re-read as an articulate and multiform testimony of the definitively anti-idolatrous meaning of the profession of Christological faith. Taking advantage precisely of the paradox of the messianic identity of the man crucified and risen from the dead *in accordance with the Scriptures* (cf. 1 Cor 15:3-5), this implied the radical negation of any triumphalist and violent interpretation of the identity of 'people of God' and of the figure of the one who would guarantee its messianic restoration; at the same time, it implied the theoretical and practical proclamation of unity and reconciliation between men and women beyond the hurt of every antithesis of a cultural, social and ethnic-religious origin (cf. Gal 3:28; 6:15; Eph 2:11-22; Col 3:11). In this sense it may be said that the first Christians, understanding themselves as God's messianic people, heirs of the blessings of Abraham and of the rights of Israel, also gave to the notion of people a 'political' connotation, tending to interpret it – in the most disparate ways, by view of the concrete and specific contexts of life in the different *ekklēsiai* – with faithfulness to the revolution of values inherent in the preaching of the Kingdom of God of Jesus of Nazareth and signified in his life-practice in defence of and as a ransom for the most fragile social and political categories. Culturally placed in the social and political context of the Roman Empire – and, probably, not always satisfactory in all its outcomes – even theirs appears as a strenuous and open struggle for liberation in the path traced by a

Messiah remembered as obviously 'popular' (cf. Matt 26:5 // Mk 14:2; Lk 19:47-48; 20:19; 21:37-38) but profoundly distant both from an idolatrous and imperialist interpretation of his own identity on the part of the people (cf. Jn 6:14-15) and from the arrogant and patronising dissociation from the hopes of the people on the part of its leaders (cf. Gv 7:49: 'but this crowd, which does not know the law, they are accursed').

Among the different post-Christian expressions of this anti-idolatrous struggle for liberation, there are two which it seems to me to be particularly useful to call to mind in this context: one contained in 1 Peter and one contained in the book of Revelation, both texts in which the Christological re-configuration of the identity of the people of God stands out in the socio-political, cultural, economic and religious context of the Roman Empire. In 1 Peter the word which expresses the identity of the messianic people is now the 'brotherhood' (*adelphotēs*, cf. 1 Pet 2:17; 5:9),[21] the 'household of God' (cf. 1 Pet 4:17) of those without social houses who, in the Asiatic cities of the Roman Empire, reside as 'resident foreigners' or 'exiles' in the diaspora (cf. 1 Pet 1:1,17; 2:11), exposed to various kinds of oppression and social ostracism.[22] The alternative to their condition as strangers is not just a 'citizenship in heaven' (cf. Phil 3:20), but the home they find in Christian fraternity as social space of integration, identification and freedom. In an especially polemic manner, on the other hand, the prophetic book par excellence of the New Testament, Revelation (cf. Rev 1:3; 22:10, 18), re-writes the Exodus Christologically and represents the anti-idolatrous challenge thrown out to the seven churches of Asia by the prophet John. In Revelation, the identity construct of the messianic people, in the 'local discourse' [23] which the book represents, is the fruit of an unrelenting fight against the idolatry of a totalitarian power in all its political, economic and cultic forms and expressions (cf. Rev 13). Against this form of idolatry, which sums up every type of infidelity and identity failure, the churches must fight and triumph by remaining faithful, even unto death (cf. Rev 2:10; 6:9-11; 12:11; 13:15; 20:4), to Christ the Lamb, royal and victorious leader but with garments drenched in blood (cf. Rev 5; 7:14; 19:11-16). The fruit of their fight, if victorious, is the dissolution of Babylon, the bloodthirsty city (cf. Rev 17:5-6; 18:24), and the total manifestation of the heavenly Jerusalem, the holy city. With perfect and well-defined boundaries, it nevertheless has its twelve doors always open (Rev 21:25); on them are written the names of the twelve tribes of Israel (Rev 21:12), but the people which comprise it are now people from 'every nation, from all tribes and peoples and languages' (Rev 7:9), a formula which calls to mind the Genesis language, and which, with its seven occurrences in the book (cf. also Rev 5:9; 10:11; 11:9; 13:7; 14:6; 17:15), indicates that the sovereignty of God and the Lamb is exercised effectively over all the nations of the world. The identity of the people of God within the city is now realised inclusively and universally, in the plural (cf. Rev 21:3); worship is celebrated in it but without the Temple (Rev 21:22); and God reigns with no further need to master anyone (22:5), no longer inflicting and experiencing oppression and death (Rev 21:4).[24] The Christological prophecy of the Kingdom, the ultimate interpretation of the whole of the Law, no longer leaves any room for idols or the lethal effects of idolatry; over it the identity of the people of God procedurally takes shape.

IV Conclusion

In the final analysis, Scripture, too, is aware of the dynamics which, today, we can identify as morphological constants of every populism: it speaks about them and portrays them in an exemplary fashion as possible, and historically realised, ways for the identity self-construction of a people, even of the 'people of God' with its guides. It challenges them, however, because in its prophetic DNA it makes a ruthless denunciation of them, and in the most varied ways, kaleidoscopic like a 'varied kaleidoscope', can be called populism with its different fetishes. It challenges them, above all, because in the renewal or Christological synthesis of the identity and destiny of the people of God, 'chosen' and 'anointed', it makes of its defence of the weakest and in the fight against every idolatrous and bloodthirsty government and power the surest criterion for the unmasking of the fetishes of the people and its guides. If the different forms and manifestations of what we call populism are attempts by human groups to find salvation, according to the Scriptures, this salvation can only occur in the sign of the respect of the human person and his / her diversity: not humanity or 'the people' as an abstract category, but real and differentiated individuals in the spatial-temporal tangibility of their environmental relations. Consequently, it cannot be achieved in the sign of the obsessive search for a leader or one language which does not leave room for difference and risk, but in the slow and laborious construction, contextually and conflicting, of what 'assists' communion and unity between human beings; not with the elimination of inter-human mediation but in the exaltation of the capacities of human beings to mutually correlate inclusively, taking risks, within and beyond any condition of social exposure.

Translated by Patricia Kelly

Notes

1. M. Murgia, interview in *L'Espresso* 30/7/2018. (http://espresso.repubblica.it/attualita/2018/07/18/news/i-forum-dellespressonon-abbiamo-fattoquello-chei-forum-dell-espressoi-forum-dellespresso-1.325034).
2. C. Mudde – C. Rovira Kaltwasser, Populism. A very short Introduction, Oxford University Press, Oxford 2017, 2; cf. M. Revelli, Populismo 2.0, Einaudi, Turin 2017, 4-5 but also F. Rostelli's interview with Noam Chomsky published in Il Manifesto 9 September 2018 (https://global.ilmanifesto.it/chomsky-working-people-are-turning-against-the-elites-its-not-populism/).
3. Cf. C. Mudde – C. Rovira Kaltwasser, *Populism*, 40.
4. N. Merker, *Filosofie del populismo*, Laterza, Bari 2009, 8.
5. M. Revelli, *Populismo* 2.0, 7-8.
6. N. Merker, *Filosofie*, 10-11. Cf. also p. 7.
7. Ibid., 9-10.
8. Cf. Ibid., 169-188.
9. See P. Beauchamp, *L'uno e l'altro Testamento. Saggio di lettura*, Paideia, Brescia 1985, 286.313; *L'uno e l'altro Testamento 2. Compiere le Scritture*, Glossa, Milan 2001, 366-367. 416.
10. L. Arcari, 'Identità collettive, identità etniche, identità religiose. Elementi per una trattazione nella prospettiva della *longue durée* (tra antichità e medioevo)', in *Reti Medievali Rivista*, 16, 1(2015), 37.
11. P. Beauchamp, *Leggere la Sacra Scrittura oggi*, Editrice Massimo, Milan 2007, 83.
12. L. Arcari, 'Identità', 35.
13. P. Beauchamp, *Le récit, la Lettre et le Corps*, Les Éditions du Cerf, Paris 1982, 205.
14. Ibid., 206.
15. A. Wenin, *Da Adamo ad Abramo o l'errare dell'uomo. Lettura narrativa e antropologica della Genesi*, EDB, Bologna 2008, 156.
16. Cf. Ibid., 156-157.
17. Ibid., 158.
18. P. Beauchamp, *Le récit, la Lettre et le Corps*, 208.
19. P. Beauchamp, *La legge di Dio*, Piemme, Casale Monferrato 2000, 105.
20. P. Beauchamp, *La legge di Dio*, 116-117.
21. Cf. J. Schlosser, "Aimez la fraternité' (1 P 2,17): A propos de l'ecclésiologie de la première lettre de Pierre', In Id., *À la recherche de la Parole. Études d'exégèse et de théologie biblique*, Paris, Cerf 2005, 463-481.

22. See the thesis of J.H. Elliott, *A Home for the Homeless. A Social-Scientific Criticism of 1Peter, Its Situation and Strategy*, Wipf & Stock Publishers, Eugene (OR) 20052.
23. Cf. L. Arcari, Collective cohabitations and self-definitions in the *ekklesiai* of Asia Minor at the end of the 1st century A.D. The Apocalypse of Giovanni as a 'speech' local note in urban contexts, in *La Parola del Passato. Rivista di studi antichi* LXXI/I (2016) 235-282.
24. Cf. K. Wengst, 'Babylon the Great and the New Jerusalem: The Visionary View of Political Reality in the Revelation of John', in H.G. Reventlow, Y. Hoffman and B. Uffenheimer (eds.), *Politics and Theopolitics in the Bible and Postbiblical Literature*, Sheffield Academic Press, Sheffield 1994, 189-202.

'Bridges not Barriers':
The Potential of Christian Hope to Counter Right-Wing Populism

ANDREAS LOB-HÜDEPOHL

Right-wing populist attitudes aggressively target the Establishment and in particular all those whom they dismiss and exclude because of their origin, religion or sexual orientation. Such attitudes have penetrated deep into society and the churches. They deny the fundamental equality of all human beings, which is both a promise of modern democracies and the fundamental Christian conviction that all *human beings are created in the image and likeness of God. In the face of the fear-filled visions of doom purveyed by right-wing populist attitudes, Christians and churches must bear witness to the potential of Christian hope, maintain it and demonstrate its truth by bridge-building as part of the activity of civil society. In so doing they perform the liturgical role of* pontifex *in everyday life (Rom 12.2).*

I. The 'highest' against the 'lowest'

'Populists always bring out the worst in us human beings.' This remark was made a few years ago by a holocaust survivor in a video that became famous beyond Austria, where she lives. Note that this Austrian pensioner is talking, not about a specific group, but about *all* human beings as those who can have the worst brought out of them. And she is also talking about herself. In fact, all human beings are potentially vulnerable to populist temptations. Radical changes in almost all areas of both individual life and the life of society as a whole leave no-one unaffected. Winners and losers are also very unevenly divided. Probably all of us at some time suffer painful disappointments, bitter defeats and nagging fears about the future.

That is why hardly anyone can really be proof against the temptation at least on occasion to give vent to their fears, disappointments or irritations in indignation and rage.

But instead of directing this indignation and rage – irrespective of whether it is justified or unjustified – into a constructive search for alternatives or at least into democratic protest – populists work up such fears and turn them, with hate-filled speech, against the 'establishment', against elites in politics, the economy and, more recently, in the churches, culture and the academic world. They direct their hate especially against all those who are weaker, who cannot defend themselves or who for other reasons make good 'scapegoats'. That is the particular characteristic of right-wing populism: not only does it stir up resentment against those seen as different or foreign, against people with a different religion or refugees, against the long-term unemployed or homeless, against homosexuals, transsexuals, and so on. It also dismisses these sections of the population *en masse* as less valuable. It assigns them a lower social status, which ultimately makes them people without rights. Right-wing populists deny the fundamental principle of democracy that all people are basically equal. They may call for society to show solidarity – but only among those who have always been a part of it. The aim of this excluding solidarity is protection – but against all those who don't belong and with barriers of the most varied kinds.

Among those human beings in whom right-wing populist movements bring out 'the worst' are many professing Christians and active church-goers, because for some time populism of the right has made deep inroads into society *and the churches*.[1] This cannot but be disturbing: are not exclusive forms of solidarity, social ranking and hate-filled speech diametrically opposed to genuinely Christian convictions? What about the extension of Christian love of neighbour to those who are distant on the model of the Good Samaritan? Or Paul's famous saying: 'There is no longer Jew or Greek, there is no longer slave or free, there is no longer male and female; for all of you are one in Christ Jesus' (Gal 3.28). Or the words of the prophet Isaiah: 'Do not fear, for I am with you, do not be afraid, for I am your God' (Is 41.10).

In the midst of all our irritation, we must remember: Christians are always 'children of their time'. We must appreciate the full force of the opening words of the Vatican II document *Gaudium et spes*: 'The joys and the hopes, the griefs and the anxieties of the men of this age, especially those who are poor or in any way afflicted, these are the joys and hopes, the griefs and anxieties of the followers of Christ. Indeed, nothing genuinely human fails to raise an echo in their hearts' (GS 1). There can be no doubt that among these human feelings that can constantly appear even in the hearts of the 'followers of Christ' as a result of right-populist temptations are these depths of hate and violence. And they cannot be dealt with by stressing the incompatibility of fearful rejection of anything strange with the Christian creed. Behind hate speech lie injuries and experiences of being despised that, at least from the subjective perspective of those affected, have a real core that gives them justification. They cannot simply be brushed aside. Instead these feelings must be taken seriously, but also taken as an opportunity to transform them into constructive options for action that respect our humanity. This is the view put forward in the message from the 2018 world conference on 'Xenophobia, Racism, and Populist Nationalism in the Context of Global Migration', organised jointly by the Vatican and the World Council of Churches, which openly challenged these right-wing populist movements: 'We recognize that the concerns of many individuals and communities who feel threatened by migrants –whether for security, economic or cultural identity reasons–have to be acknowledged and examined. We wish to be in genuine dialogue with all those who hold such concerns. But based upon the principles of our Christian faith and the example of Jesus Christ, we seek to raise a narrative of love and of hope, against the populist narrative of hate and of fear.'2 Here the world's Catholics and Protestants describe the specifically Christian starting-point for challenging right-wing populism: instead of the barriers and oppressive fear and angst of right-wing populism they offer the basic models of the solidarity that breaks down divisions in the form of Christian hope, the confidence that through trust in the liberating presence of the God to whom the bible testifies any attempt to overcome experiences of loss and injury makes sense even if the result of any commitment to make the world more human is not certain. This is the best that human beings imbued with hope have to offer as an alternative to the worst that can be brought out in us.

II Fear comes from deep insecurity

What are the causes of these fears that are expressed as xenophobia or other right-wing populist attitudes? People sympathetic to right-wing populism do not form a homogeneous group; they belong to the most varied social and even political groups. Key elements of right-wing populist attitudes such as 'group-specific hostility' are to be found in all established professional groups and associations, and in trade unions and parties.[3] Nonetheless apart from the leaders of right-wing populist movements and parties, who have no scruple about exploiting fear to advance their political agenda, what unites people sympathetic to right-wing populism is a deep-seated insecurity. Again the causes of this are varied. Some people feel unsettled by rapid social change. The digital world, globalisation and finally the increasing number of world crises (the financial crisis, the climate crisis) are shaking their familiar, reliable way of life to its foundations. Others feel themselves pushed out economically, socially or culturally and are afraid that when more new people and foreigners arrive things will get even worse for them. Others again feel so uneasy at foreign ways of life or religions that they imagine that their way of life will disappear and so try to fend off anything unusual with all their strength.

The decisive factor, however, is not that the economic social or even cultural situation of deeply insecure people is *in fact* precarious or under threat. What is decisive is how the people affected perceive and interpret their situation in life subjectively, in their heads. This produces the seemingly paradoxical situation that even middle-class people are seized with fear and almost panic. These people assess their own current situation as good or very good – they have a job, an adequate income, they feel well integrated into their family and social circles of friends and neighbours. And yet they are racked by a great fear for the future. They fear that their hopes and aspirations may come to naught at any minute. As soon as society's promise of a constant rise up the social scale for them or their children is not fulfilled, they fear falling into the abyss of marginality, dependence and exclusion.[4] So they long for protection – to be sealed off externally and internally to retain their group privileges, first their own people, their own culture, their own religion – even if, as in many parts of Germany, it is the religion one doesn't believe in, being an atheist, agnostic or just having 'no ear for religion', but whose features are familiar from one's surroundings and which one can keep in reserve just in case.[5] Foreigners', 'refugees' or people 'not like us' are perceived as unwelcome competition, competition for my own prosperity, competition for my chances of getting on in life or getting a position of power, competition for schools, leisure facilities and much more. Such 'social closures', as Max Weber called them', are by no means a new phenomenon. Quite the opposite: in the battle for (really or supposedly) scarce resources, members of the middle ranks of society tend generally to try to exclude and block those who might push up from below.[6]

Reactions to feelings of being threatened or treated with contempt and fears of loss may turn out to be unjustified. Perhaps they may even be simple expressions of the narrow-minded struggle to maintain egoistical privileges, and in the processes of social negotiation they will have to be rejected. On the other hand, they must be taken seriously as factors that affect political processes. Helmut Dubiel calls this crucial factor in social processes 'political subjectivity'. By this he means the 'potential moral factors that are supposed not only to give outward legitimation to the adoption of a political attitude or the formation of an opinion, but also steer them at the deeper levels of the individual psyche'. Political subjectivity includes 'the expectations of happiness, claims to justice, needs for social recognition and cultural identity that on the whole lie below everyday consciousness' and which in times of social change and uncertainty are expressed in inverted form 'as a feeling of justice denied, slights to social status, a sense of withheld happiness' and so on.[7]

III. 'Do not be afraid...' – for political subjectivity imbued with hope

The crucial question is how such political subjectivity can be transformed in a way that makes it compatible with humane values – at least wherever it is used by right-wing populism to damage and undermine the life chances of others in order to consolidate one's own. In this transformation to promote humane values Christians and churches have a key asset in their God language and faith convictions, which can be a crucial factor in influencing subjectivity relevant to politics: the hope and trust in the ultimately saving and healing presence of God that breaks down barriers and instead builds bridges in order to bring together what has been divided and damagingly fragmented.

A caveat: such hope and trust is neither obvious, nor does it give impregnable security. Christian hope produces confidence, not certainty. It blocks out the attitudes normally associated with expectations and plans.

Normal human hopes reflect expectations of a future that human beings try to anticipate with predictions and plans. Christian hope, in contrast, is 'hoping against hope' (Rom 4.18). It has its foundation and origin in the God of the Christian faith. It comes to human beings as a gift. It is beyond our control. It cannot be included as a fixed item in our plans. It happens where God is to be; it often happens when we have stopped expecting it. It is not available without its uncertainty and approximation – precisely because it promises salvation from the God who is beyond our control.[8] This uncertainty is sometimes hard to bear. The emergence of apocalyptic literature in Judaism around in the second century BCE – the book of Daniel is an example – is impressive evidence of this. The failure of the 'new earth' promised by God to arrive turns into a longing for the dramatic end of a history increasingly felt to be malign and ruined. God himself will put bring this history to an end by demonstrating his power and destroying the old world and so definitively establish his rule.[9]

Apocalyptic attitudes of this sort are also not at all foreign to the early Jesus movement. With the book of Revelation they found their way into the canon of scripture as a blazing full stop to biblical narratives. In addition, they led to a more complex sense of the kingdom of God. God's reign has come near and dawned in and through Jesus Christ; it is now completely a reality, but not yet complete reality.[10] It is waiting for its completion at the end of time. Nevertheless, it is already taking shape here and now in the actions of those who, as disciples of Jesus Christ, motivated and guided by his Spirit, make his unconditional desire for peace and justice luminous to all people in the quality of community life. The reality of the redemptive and liberating closeness of God becomes present in those encounters and attempts to build community in which people transmit to their fellow human beings the life-affirming effectiveness of joining together in solidarity. This unity may constantly be limited by the ever-present danger of fragmentation, but nevertheless through the potential fragmentation can be seen the first glimmer of the absolute desire, recognition and acceptance that is the destiny of *all* – despite whatever differences and distinctions that may exist between human beings in terms of gender, origin, religious or political convictions, etc. In this activity 'salvation from God for human beings' is made present.[11] 'The fact that human beings may make present without having to exhaust it – that is the essence of Christian freedom and the basis of its hope, the historical reality of redemption.'[12] Putting

Christian hope into practice in this way has a solid foundation. While it may point towards something that ultimately is not certain, but can only be hoped for, it is definitely more than a sentimental longing that cannot cope with existing conditions and so keeping looking out for something else. Christian hope builds on the foundation of the raising of Jesus from the dead. The raising of Jesus is evidence of the unbreakable solidarity of his Father, who keeps faith with him in and through death. It is also evidence that the life-affirming message of Jesus in no way suffered final annihilation in death on the cross, but survived and lives on. Christian hope thus transmits the confidence that all the works 'of justice and peace done in human history in the power of his Spirit',[13] being done today and those that will be done again in the future, are enduring, that nothing of them can any longer be completely removed from the world. Seen in this way, Christian hope in no sense denies the defeats and disappointments people can suffer in the course of their lives. But it creates a confidence in life that can leave its mark as an essential element not only of efforts to create a private life, but also take up a position in the 'political subjectivity' of a person's life and from there stimulate and enrich a constructive approach to the fears and insecurities that arise in society.

IV. 'A people made up of peoples' – against attempts by the populist right to usurp Christianity

Christian hope has a fundamentally positive stance that leads it to reject all apocalyptic visions of doom issuing from a nihilistic hermeneutics of suspicion. Nevertheless, this characteristic that pervades Christian existence and the Church's sense of Christian identity has not been able to prevent the penetration of right populist temptations into the 'hearts' and 'heads' of a considerable number of the 'Christian faithful'. One reason for this may be that, while Christian hope is quite clear, other Christian religious traditions present in the right populist environment seem – at least at first sight – to offer points of contact with Christian senses of identity and elements of tradition and so threaten to counter the Christian message of hope that transcends all boundaries.

One example of this is the Church's understanding of itself as the people of God and the populist insinuation that a people is an ethnic unity. The right populists' cleverly formulated question asks, Don't all 'peoples of God' claim the right to a form of selection and a degree of exclusivity that exclude all those who do not belong from the range of their solidarity and attention, when they do not systematically treat them as less valuable? Can Christians credibly distance themselves from the various forms of rejection and exclusion involved in the call to belong to a particular people when as the Church they form a people of their own? Is not the territory of the (right-wing) populist appeal to the people as a more or less homogeneous *ethnos* at least formally very close to the identity of the Christian Church, with the result that there is a cultural bridge that makes both sides prepared to amalgamate?

It is true that the identity the Church attributes to itself as the people of God comes initially from the tradition of ancient Judaism, which was bound by an understanding of a 'people' in terms of physical descent, in other words, *ethnos*. And to denote the 'people of God' the primitive Christian literature itself uses the Greek term *laos theou*, from which we get the term 'laity'.[14] Instead of having the connotation of (simple) 'lay people' in contrast to the (knowledgeable) 'experts', however, the New Testament tradition uses the *term laos* as an honorific title. It stands for membership of those who form the living body of Christ. And membership of this body of Christ – another biblical image for those inspired by the Spirit of God and called together in the *ecclesia* ('Church') – includes not only those who can belong to it as Jews by descent. Very early, possibly while the preacher from Nazareth was still alive, but certainly with the theological success of *Paul*, who famously, with his so-called 'mission to the gentiles', was able to impose himself against the position attributed to Peter, of limiting access to the Christian communities exclusively to adherents of Judaism, and step by step established the principle that membership of the Church of Jesus Christ was universal, irrespective of the origin, the status, the sex or other distinctions that previously had been significant. This is precisely what is meant by the Pauline formula: 'There is no longer Jew or Greek, there is no longer slave or free, there is no longer male and female; for all of you are one in Christ Jesus' (Gal 3.28).

Naturally all the distinctions between the genders, between social statuses or between those descended from different religions or races, did not fall away. What did fall away were the barriers that helped to reinforce the normal distinctions of status. Possibly Jesus the Jew initially intended to promote an internal Jewish renewal movement, but his behaviour described in the tradition shows unequivocally the tendency of his message to present salvation as universal. And the diversity of his supporters, who, as it were, moved towards becoming – not without challenge – the face of the Jesus movement, demonstrates this impressively: zealots and customs officers – otherwise fiercely hostile to each other –, 'religious people' and 'whores'. The unity of the Jesus movement was never the product of the uniformity of Jesus' supporters, but in the univocal liberating message he brought and in readiness for discipleship at almost any cost.

In this tradition the Church of Christ has never been a homogeneous community, but always a diverse people, consisting of many different peoples. It is true that Christianity has always had difficulty with this. Even today the Roman Catholic Church in particular in many aspects of its life prizes imposed uniformity over unified diversity. Nevertheless at least since the Second Vatican Council it thinks of itself as a 'people made up of different peoples', whose unity appears in diversity. This 'people made up of different peoples' in the narrow sense is indeed made up only of the baptised and confirmed. In this sense membership is limited. But the saving mission, of which this circumscribed *laos theou* is intended to be the starting point, is certainly not limited to itself. On the contrary, in the story of the Good Samaritan, the preacher from Nazareth himself removed all barriers from responsibility for helping people in distress. It is this responsibility that defines the range of attention inspired by solidarity and imbued with hope, and not any considerations of descent or social connections.

V Christian hope as a commitment to building bridges

As we have seen, Christian talk of the 'people of God' rejects any attempt at making a parallel with the populists' 'people' as a (homogeneous) *ethnos* to give it legitimacy. Similarly, it can also reject all other populist attempts to latch on to elements of the Christian tradition or even to occupy it in order to promote its own agenda. It can do this from a position of clear opposition to the most frequent populist attitudes and set itself up as a bulwark against all attempts to take over Christian concepts: this is the capacity for resistance of hope in practice.

Admittedly, the term 'bulwark' could encourage the misunderstanding that the capacity for resistance in Christian hope really means putting up new walls and barriers to shelter behind while keeping others at a distance. But it would only get into this self-contradictory position if it neglected a commitment to removing barriers and removing fears in the structures of ordinary life in the world and to give an account of the hope that is alive in Christians (cf *Lumen Gentium*, 35). A commitment to remove barriers and fears is a practical application of Christian trust in God in the places where people live their lives and in the quarrels of everyday life.

A particularly appropriate range of opportunities to give account of Christian hope today is involvement in civil society.[15] The potential of sectors of civil society in the combat against populist movements and temptations can be seen from the varied experiences of a civil society culture involving argument, protest, but also compromise. Involvement in civil society uses the existing resources of citizens in an area and seeks to develop them in such a way that even negative experiences of 'political subjectivity' can be transformed into constructive attitudes and actions. Neighbourhoods usually contain much potential for conflict. They have within them as many different attitudes as there are different people living (forced to live) in them. Nevertheless, their key advantage is that involvement in civil society can use these spaces to overcome the barriers between groups, bring different, and occasionally hostile, groups together and build both social and mental bridges. Such efforts at connecting and bridge-building makes it possible to look for solutions together – even if they are at first initial compromises that have to be constantly revisited, renewed and repaired. But every effort to reach a compromise generates a pull that can soften attitudes and mentalities just as they are beginning to harden, dismantle barriers and produce a constructive outlook.

This connecting and bridge-building does not require a religious faith. Nevertheless, Christians and churches do possess a responsibility, not only for strengthening political culture, but above all for injecting hope into religious subjectivity to make it that model of interpretation that foreshadows both a person's basic attitude to the world and their action in it. There can be no doubt that one authentic area for action is the promotion of inter-religious dialogue – not only between leaders, but also directly between people of faith in the neighbourhood. Inter-religious learning does not just increase intercultural skills in general, but at its heart is curiosity for something that transcends what I already have. It depends on prioritising questions rather than pat answers. Inter-religious learning illustrates the tension that is at the heart of Christian hope – confidence, yes, but no easy certainty.

The Potential of Christian Hope to Counter Right-Wing Populism

And in addition Christian hope could inspire the building of a particular sort of bridges, solidarity with people who for whatever reason have fallen victim to right-wing populist activists. Solidarity here does not mean, like the (right-wing) populists, to adopt or even encourage defensive attitudes and fears of loss. What solidarity means in these cases is to take up justified fears and reasons for anger in order to refer them democratically, that is, in open discussion, to those who hold political responsibility – or, where they are unjustified, courageously to challenge their sources. This form of solidarity shows that both individual Christians and churches are needed as part of the civil society conversation. Here they share with all the others involved the task of encouraging the formation of positive opinions and attitudes, to accompany these processes critically and also to lead them. In this way they can show that they are the sort of people who are indispensable to building bridges across all social and mental barriers or, in ecclesiological terms, real symbolic bridge-builders – performing the office of *pontifex* – in the world as it is (cf Rom 12.2).

Translated by Francis McDonagh

Notes

1. For Germany see Oliver Decker, Johannes Kiess, Elmar Brähler (ed.): *Die stablisierte Mitte: Rechtsextreme Einstellungen in Deutschland*, Leipzig, 2014; Werner Fröhlich, Christian Ganser, Eva Köhler, *Gruppenbezogene Menschenfeindlichkeit* in Bayern, Munich, 2016; Andreas Lob-Hüdepohl, 'Verdeckte und offene Xenophobien in Gesellschaft und Kirche. Anmerkungen aus theologisch-ethischer Perspektive', *Ökumenische Rundschau* 66, (2/2017), 237-245.
2. Message from the Conference 'Xenophobia, Racism and Populist Nationalism in the Context of Global Migration' organized jointly by the Dicastery for Promoting Integral Human Development (Vatican City) and the World Council of Churches (Geneva) in collaboration with the Pontifical Council For Promoting Christian Unity (Vatican City), Rome,18-20 September 2018, para 8b: http://www.humandevelopment.va/content/dam/sviluppoumano/eventi/convegno-xenophobia/Xenorac2018-Final%20Message.pdf
3. See the so-called Leipzig 'middle studies', under way since 2002, most recently Andreas Zick et al., (ed.), *Gespaltene Mitte. Feindselige Zustände. Rechtsextreme Einstellungen in Deutschland 2016*, Bonn, 2016.
4. See Oliver Nachtwei, *Die Abstiegsgesellschaft. Über das Aufbegehren in der regressiven Moderne*, Berlin, 2017, pp 119ff.
5. Given this, it is not surprising that the 'defenders of the Christian West against the threat of Islam' have been most successful where the population is made up of a mere 20% of Christians and 0.4% of Muslims, but 80% declaring 'no religion'.

6. See Karin Priester, *Rechter und linker Populismus. Annäherung an ein Chamäleon*, Frankfurt am Main, 2012, pp 20-21.
7. Helmut Dubiel, 'Das Gespenst des Populismus', Dubiel (ed.): *Populismus und Aufklärung*, Frankfurt am Main, 1986, pp 33-50, quotation p. 47.
8. See Karl Rahner: 'Zur Theologie der Hoffnung', *Schriften zur Theologie*, vol. 8, Einsiedeln, 1967, pp 561-579, quotation, p. 576.
9. See Karlheinz Müller, 'Apokalyptik I. Geschichtliche Entwicklung der frühjüdischen Antike', *Lexikon für Theologie und Kirche* 1, 1993, pp 814-818.
10. See Jürgen Ebach, 'Eschatologie/Apokalypse', Peter Eicher, *NHthG* 1, Munich, new ed., 2005, pp 260-272.
11. See Edvard Schillebeeckx, *Christus und die Christen. Geschichte einer neuen Lebenspraxis*. Freiburg am Breisgau, 1977.
12. Thomas Pröppe, E*rlösungsglaube und Freiheitsgeschichte. Eine Skizze zur Soteriologie*, Munich, 2nd ed, substantially expanded, 1988, p.210.
13. Medard Kehl, *Eschatologie*, Würzburg, 2nd ed., 1988, p.218
14. See Wolfgang Kraus, article 'Volk Gottes. Biblisch-theologisch: 2. Neues Testament', *Lexikon für Theologie und Kirche* X (2001), pp 846-847.
15. I have gone into this in more detail in: Andreas Lob-Hüdepohl, 'Demokratie stark machen gegen Rechtspopulismus – auch ein Beitrag der Kirchen', in Sonja Angelika Strube (ed.): *Das Fremde akzeptieren. Gruppenbezogener Menschenfeindlichkeit entgegenwirken. Theologische Ansätze*, Freiburg im Breisgau, 2017, pp 123-137.

Right-wing Populism and Catholicity: An Ecclesiological Reflection

FRANZ GMAINER-PRANZEL

If the Christian churches are to engage with right-wing populism, they need to reflect on ecclesiology. The Vatican II Dogmatic Constitution on the Church, Lumen Gentium, sets out in section 13 its understanding of catholicity, which differs fundamentally from identitarian ideas in the following features: its reference to the unity of the whole of humanity, the formation of the 'people of God' by a call and not through 'birth', willingness to learn from strangers and what is strange, the internal plurality of the Church, the understanding of sacramentality as 'relatedness', concern for the salvation of all people ('recapitulation'), and a future-oriented understanding of 'homeland'. On this basis a new 'courage to be Catholic' can offer a creative alternative to right-wing populist attitudes.

'Right-wing populism' has become a ubiquitous term, in debates in both political science and theology. In this it reflects a development that even a short time ago would have been hardly imaginable: neo-authoritarian, identitarian, xenophobic and nationalist language are present in the government programmes of several European countries and have reached 'the heart of society'. This collective swing to the right has also shaken theology in the German-speaking countries – and not only there – and initiated an intensive debate with right-wing populism,1 which has been reinforced considerably by Pope Francis' pontificate and his pleas for social justice, a humane asylum policy and a recognition of the value of cultural diversity. But this commitment should not blind us to the fact that a firm critique of (right-wing) populist politics is still a minority interest in the Church. Political conflicts in the 19th and 20th centuries led to a rejection in many parts of the Catholic Church, especially in continental Europe, of liberal or social democratic positions that persists so rigidly that considerable numbers of Catholics in Europe tend to sympathise with right-wing ideas in social policy. There is also an inflationary tendency in discussions of right-wing populism that leaves the meaning of the term vague; on the one hand, every nationalist cliché or authoritarian attitude from a politician in itself a sign of a right-populist programme, while on the other populist politics has to be distinguished from right-wing extremism.[2]

In the light of this, efforts to achieve a clearer understanding of what is commonly known as 'right-wing populism' such as those undertaken by, for example, Jan-Werner Müller or Ruth Wodak are very welcome. Populisms, Müller says, are above all anti-pluralistic; they claim to represent the 'true people', exclusively and directly. The real diversity and heterogeneity of society does not count, but an ideal homogeneity, which is represented symbolically – and whoever does not identify with this 'people' is classed as part of the 'elites' or the 'opposition'.[3] Ruth Wodak, too, shows in her analysis that the key point of (right-wing) populist strategies, apart from personalising, polarising and injecting emotion into political activity, is the construction of '*the* people', which is imagined in nativist and cultural terms and defended through a rhetoric of fear.[4] For theology this essentialist, binary and ultimately totalitarian language is extremely relevant when this 'true people' is identified with Christianity, or when a society is regarded as 'Christian' when it appears to be culturally and religiously most homogeneous – like a European or North American cultural Christianity, which stresses its difference especially from Islam. The idea of the 'Christian West', which is evoked in this way – and always as a concept for use *against* others, not as an inspiration for a common enterprise – shows itself on closer inspection to be a myth, adapted to whatever are the current political interests.[5] This instrumentalising of ideas with a Christian brand to serve an identitarian politics must give theology pause and lead it to a self-critical reflection on its own understanding of Church and society, religion and politics, identity and plurality. The reflections in this article (1) start from a consideration of the influence of identitarian ideas on the Christian churches' views of themselves, (2) examine the fundamental differences between the concepts of right-wing populism and Catholicity in the light of *Lumen*

Gentium 13, and (3) outline possible perspectives for a Christian debate with right-wing populist language. The theological thesis underpinning these thoughts is the conviction that a Christianity that misunderstands its 'Catholicity' is not only helpless in the face of (right-wing) populist pressure, but ultimately loses its soul.[6]

I Is the 'clash of civilisations' the new 'grand narrative'?

Right-wing populist politics, which are essentially marked by the idea of helping the 'true people' to recover their rights, defend them against 'oppression by the elites' and 'threats from outsiders' to be their exclusive representatives, live by the power of cultural identities. What counts here is not *demos* but *ethnos*, as Jürgen Habermas put it in his diagnosis of right-wing currents at the end of the 20th century: 'The 'we-consciousness', founded on an imagined blood relation or on cultural identity, of people who share a belief in a common origin, identify one another as 'members' of the same community, and thereby set themselves apart from their environment, is supposed to constitute the *common* core of the ethnic *and* of national social formations.'[7] The political violence that results from such a concept of cultural identity became visible in the 1990s in the war, or civil war, in splintering Yugoslavia, as a murderous battle against those who were presented as culturally or religiously 'different' and the creation of identities that only a few years before had been irrelevant.

It is well known that the war in Yugoslavia, with its burden of ethnic and religious feeling, was a key motive that led the US political scientist Samuel Huntington (1927-2008) to publish his book *Clash of Civilizations* (1996), an expansion of his article in the journal *Foreign Affairs*, which created great interest at the time.[9] The central thesis of his book, the diagnosis of a switch from a world determined by political ideologies to one marked by cultural affiliations can be understood today as the perception of the beginning of a right-wing populist trend: 'Culture and cultural identities, which at the broadest level are civilisation identities, are shaping the patterns of cohesion, disintegration and conflict in the post-Cold War world.'[10] While Huntington's essentialist understanding of 'culture, 'cultural circles' and 'religions' has been subjected to a robust critique, as has his antagonistic model of 'fault line conflicts',[11] and his pessimistic anthropology,[12] his analysis, however crude and polarising, did strike a nerve at the time. In times of change and lack of orientation people look for 'strong identities', and with the disappearance of the tension between the communist Eastern bloc and the capitalist Western bloc they evidently find them in membership of cultural collectivities. 'Political boundaries,' says Huntington, increasingly are redrawn to coincide with cultural ones: ethnic, religious and civilizational.'[13]

This redefinition of identities and affiliations did not leave religious communities unaffected – quite the reverse. From the final years of the 20th century, there has been an amalgamation in discourse of cultural traditions and religious beliefs that has led to unheard-of inclusion and exclusions. This could be the classification of population groups in the former Yugoslavia as belonging to particular religious communities ('Orthodox Serbs', 'Catholic Croats', 'Muslim Bosnians') or the automatic attribution of a 'Muslim identity' to migrants and their children.[14] What became increasingly relevant for public discourse was neither people's social situation nor their political convictions, but exclusively their 'culture', which was often treated as identical with 'religion'. The definition of human life in terms of 'cultural identities' and the resulting 'clash of cultures' seems to have become the new 'grand narrative' of the early 21st century on which individual right-wing populist projects in several European countries – and beyond – are feeding. How far various religious communities have been drawn into this identitarian current, or have themselves contributed to such cultural and religious inclusion and exclusion will no doubt be the subject of future research into the origin of right-wing populism. Even now, however, Catholic theology needs to discuss (self-)critically those ambitions visible within the Catholic Church that hope that a coalition with right-wing populist forces in a sort of cultural politics will being them a strengthening of traditional Church identities. Some people believe that adopting right-wing positions (a reduction in the rate of migration, islamophobic rhetoric, attacking policies favouring solidarity and emancipation as 'left-wing extremism', propagating opposition to 'gender ideology') will provide an opportunity to impose or restore supposedly 'Catholic values' with the help of right-wing populist politicians. This can lead to a situation in which a number of bishops are closer to the xenophobic remarks of politicians in their own countries than to Pope Francis' plea for a culture of hospitality and welcoming refugees. Such a situation of extreme polarisation in the Church and theology leads unavoidably to the question of what position the Church should adopt in the face of culturalist, identitarian, and nationalist language – and not simply in terms of moral advice, but at a much more fundamental level. What is the Church's position in relation to the worldview, the view of humanity and the understanding of politics represented by right-wing populism? Does it share the 'grand narrative' of the *Clash of Civilizations*, or does it have its own story to tell, a counter-narrative? What basis will it find for its criticism of xenophobia, neo-authoritarian politics and the definition of social problems in cultural terms that will not come across as further patronising rather than as an expression of what the Church is and believes?

II Stamped with the 'character of universality': a demanding mission

The relatively unknown section 13 of the Vatican II Constitution on the Church, *Lumen Gentium*, presents an innovative phenomenology of catholicity, in which theological perspectives, intercultural relationships and institutional reflections are intertwined in a striking way. In the second paragraph of this text, dealing with the 'people of God', this chapter is designed to prepare for the reflections in sections 14-16 on who belongs to this 'people of God' by a careful analysis of the Church's internal structure and its relationship to the world. There are four themes in this paragraph: (1) the relationship to the whole of humanity, which, as in *Gaudium et spes* 1-3, *Nostra Aetate* 1 and *Ad Gentes* 1, as also at the beginning of *Lumen Gentium* (1) is presented as defining the Church's mission: 'All are called to belong to the new people of God' (LG 13, para 1). (2) a particular form of community life in the Church that, as a people 'made up of different peoples', does not consist of competition, cultural colonisation or assimilating globalisation, but in relationships of mutual recognition and learning. (3) the *character of universality* (*universalitatis character*), which becomes the structuring principle of the universal Church and its multiple relationships with different peoples and groups; and (4) the resulting global way of life consisting of 'fullness in unity', to be distinguished both from a centralised model of organisation and existence side by side without any relationship.

From these themes it is possible to derive seven characteristics that define more closely the life form, structure and potential for relationships of 'catholicity' and provide a clear contrasting model to those models of life and politics classed as 'right-wing populism'. When 'catholicity' is suggested here, in the light of the ecclesiological phenomenology of *Lumen Gentium* 13, as an alternative to the model of 'right-wing populism', it is important to note that the term is not understood as an exclusive denominational identifier of the Roman Catholic Church, but as a feature of every Christian church that regards itself as at the service of humankind and is also prepared to let itself be challenged and changed by the diversity of that humankind. 'Catholicity' is also understood here as a claim – in the awareness that the Roman Catholic Church too does not always resist the temptations to nationalist, xenophobic and identitarian ways of thinking. Finally, this is not a simple condemnation of right-wing populism, as though the Church could decide from on high which social currents should be accepted and which rejected.[15] In fact, there is a need for self-criticism: 'catholicity' is not a decoration the Church awards itself, but a challenge to the whole Church community. A critique of right-wing populism that does not first ask whether our own Church structures meet the demands of catholicity is not credible. In other words, only on the basis of a lived testimony of Christian faith in the perspective of its catholicity does a critical engagement with right-wing populism make sense.

In the light of this, we can identify seven characteristics of what is 'catholic' – in contrast to right-wing populism's identity politics: (1) the Church is always at the service of the *unity of the human race*. It does not advocate a separatist multi-culturalism that allows each 'culture' its own 'space', as many 'anti-migration' positions do, but works for peace and reconciliation at local and global level. (2) As a 'people' (the people of God), the Church does not regard itself as an 'ethnic group', but as a 'congregation'. No-one is 'born' into this community, but 'called'; through this call people come together (*congregare* is the term in LG 13.1) for unity. Even when the children of Catholic parents are naturally in a sense 'born into' their faith community, theologically this in no sense allows the conclusion that the 'people' of the Church are a 'national people'. They are always a 'people made up of all peoples' in whose local cultural features – which of course deserve to be respected and promoted – that 'newness of life' (*Ad gentes* 21.3) is active and gives the Church the features of a 'congregation', an *ek-klesia* and not just an *ethnos*. (3) It follows that the universal Church does not dissolve the cultural identities of the different peoples, but promotes them; it goes further, and introduces them into processes of adoption, purification and enrichment; in other words, it meets strangers *responsively* and not in terms of identity. Being 'Catholic' always also means allowing oneself to be challenged by what is new and alien and finding a response to it, not insisting on an identity that is closed to anything unusual and surprising.[16] In this sense Felix Wilfred talks of 'upside down catholicity' as a 'process of becoming universal through receiving and learning from others'[17] – in contrast to an 'expansive catholicity' that exports its own self-image throughout the world. (4) Catholicity regards plurality not only as an unavoidable necessity, but as an inner enrichment. The 'people of God' is gathered, as *Lumen Gentium* 13.3 admits with great naturalness, 'formed of different peoples' and 'it is composed of various ranks'. The 'legitimate differences' and 'special gifts' not only do not damage the unity of the Church as a whole but, on the contrary 'serve' it; *catholicitas* means that 'through the common sharing of gifts and through the common effort to attain fullness in unity, the whole and each of the parts receive increase' (13.3).[18] Being a universal Church does not mean a centralising crushing of differences, but the experience of living a form of deeper connection and unity in a great diversity'.[19] (5) The relationship between the 'people of God' and humanity is *sacramental* in structure, not totalitarian, which means that the Church, as the introduction to the Vatican II Constitution on the Church says, 'a sign and instrument ...of the unity of the whole human race' (LG 1), but it does not regard itself as the only possible or complete representation of the human race. Even if it thinks of itself as a 'universal Church', the Church knows that it can only ever represent this world fragmentarily; rejecting all the tendencies to develop an ecclesiology of the *societas perfecta*, the sacramental understanding of the Church takes the limits of institutional identity and representational capacity seriously. The Church cannot and need not represent any 'totality'; it is enough if, as *Lumen Gentium* 1 beautifully puts it, that 'light' is reflected from it that enlightens all people. (6) If the Church is aware that as the 'people of God' it is inherently limited and has no control over 'the whole', this does not mean that the horizon of her catholicity is limited. *Lumen Gentium* 13.2 mentions the idea of 'recapitulation' from Irenaeus of Lyon's *Adversus haereses* to emphasise that the Church seeks to 'sum up' (*recapitulandam*) 'the whole of humanity in the unity of Christ's Spirit.[20] This is no ethnically based Church or a Church that feels linked exclusively to particular classes, strata, environments or particular groups, but a Church that is concerned with the whole human family. It is not restriction, but recapitulation, which should be characteristic of the action of the Church of Jesus Christ, a passionate concern for all people, whatever culture, society, ethnic group, social class or religion they belong to. If 'Catholic' was taken to mean a sector of society, instead of the claim to take on the 'joys and the hopes, the griefs and the anxieties of the people of this age' (*Gaudium et spes*, 1), then the Church would run a serious risk of being absorbed by a right-wing populist agenda that is not interested in global responsibility but narrow national interests. (7) Finally we also find a different view of 'homeland' – a core category for right-wing populism – set out in *Lumen Gentium* 13. The members of the 'people of God', who naturally also belong to specific cultural traditions, ethnic communities and nation states, are also 'citizens of a kingdom which is of a heavenly rather than of an earthly nature' (Lumen Gentium 13.2); in other words, they belong to a community whose 'homeland' is essentially not based on ethnicity or nationality. In this 'people of God' Christians are on a journey towards 'fullness of life'. The Christian understanding of 'homeland' is future-oriented, whereas the right-wing populist idea is based on clinging to an (imagined) past. It is not an attempt to restore past forms of culture and ways of life that is typical of a Catholic understanding of 'homeland', but hope for 'the city that is to come' (Heb 13.14).

III Renewed courage to be Catholic

How right-wing populist forms of politics develop in the future cannot be a matter of indifference to the Christian churches, driven as they are by faith in Jesus Christ to work for a society based on solidarity, justice and humanity. It is therefore no accident that in a range of countries tensions, if not conflicts, emerge between Christian churches and politicians who adopt right-wing populist positions; these cannot be concealed by the invention of 'Christian politics' or by the sympathies that do exist within the Church for a neo-authoritarian, xenophobic and identitarian course. One important piece of learning for the churches could come from a (self-) critical reflection on the potential for 'catholicity' displayed by a 'universal Church'. Here the stimulus of *Lumen Gentium* 13 could encourage a new 'courage to be Catholic', which does not mean just organising against right-wing populism, but an attitude of hope, based on the liberating power of the Gospel to change us, towards the enriching and challenging diversity of this world. This 'courage to be Catholic' can encourage the faithful of different churches to contribute to the further development of an open society inspired by solidarity, and people active in political parties, civil society movements and NGOs to work together on solutions for the questions and challenges of our time. No to a world dominated by fear, culture wars and politics based on emotion – another world is possible.

Translated by Francis McDonagh

Notes

1. See Walter Lesch (ed.), *Christentum und Populismus. Klare Fronten?* Freiburg im Breisgau, 2017; Stefan Orth and Volker Resing (ed.), AfD, *Pegida und Co. Angriff auf die Religion?* Freiburg im Breisgau, 2017; Sonja Angelika Strube (ed.), *Das Fremde akzeptieren. Gruppenbezogener Menschenfeindlichkeit entgegenwirken. Theologische Ansätze*, Freiburg im Breisgau, 2017.
2. See Sonja Angelika Strube (Ed.), *Rechtsextremismus als Herausforderung für die Theologie*, Freiburg im Breisgau, 2015.
3. See Jan-Werner Müller, *Was ist Populismus? Ein Essay*, Berlin, 2016, pp 129, 135.
4. See Ruth Wodak, *Politik mit der Angst. Zur Wirkung rechtspopulistischer Diskurse*, Vienna and Hamburg, 2016, pp 40 42, 82 84.
5. On the various, constantly shifting meanings of 'Christian West', see Volker Weiß, *Die autoritäre Revolte. Die Neue Rechte und der Untergang des Abendlandes*, Stuttgart, 2017, pp 155 and 186.
6. See the analysis of 'Catholic' in Klaus Vechtel SJ, 'Das Katholische als Herausforderung. Überlegungen zur gegenwärtigen theologischen Diskussion um die Kirche', *ThPh* 90 (2015), 60 82; 81: 'The Church is catholic because it wants to communicate God's salvation to all, not just to an intellectual or spiritual elite, but in particular to sinners, ordinary people, the poor and excluded, the doubters and seekers. The concept 'catholic' becomes divisive when God's offer of salvation is restricted to a few, where a church is formed of a select group, those who are better, pure. The challenge of being Catholic consists in understanding ourselves, even while being a 'little flock', not as an exclusive counter-culture in a moment of crisis.
7. Jürgen Habermas,'On the Relation between the Nation, the Rule of Law and Democracy', *The Inclusion of the Other. Studies in Political Theory*, Chicago IL, and London, 1999, pp 129-154.
8. 'The assumption of the existence of an inaccessible collective identity creates a drive for repressive politics, whether the compulsory assimilation of alien elements or maintain the purity of the people through apartheid and ethnic cleansing' (Habermas, ibid.)
9. Samuel P. Huntington, 'The Clash of Civilizations?' Foreign Affairs 72 (1993), 3, 22 49. The question mark Huntington placed at the end of the title of his article (which was absent from the book title) led a number of commentators to speculate that Huntington himself initially had doubts about his thesis of a battle of cultures
10. Samuel P. Huntington, *The Clash of Civilizations and Remaking of World Order*, London and New York, 1997.

11. 'In fault line conflicts either side has reasons not only to defend its own cultural identity but also to emphasise that of the opposing side' (Huntington, ibid.).
12. 'Hating is human. Human beings need enemies to define and motivate themselves' (ibid).
13. Huntington, *Clash of Civilisations*.
14. See, for example the moving description of the experiences of racism and exclusion that led Zacarias Moussaoui, a secular young man born in France to Moroccan immigrants, first to frustration and finally into the arms of the terrorist group responsible for the attacks of 11 September 2001: Abd Samad Moussaoui and Florence Bouquillat, *Zacarias my Brother: The Making Of A Terrorist*, London, 2003.
15. See Stefan Hermann, 'Wie politisch muss Kirche sein? Kirche und die Herausforderungen durch radikale und populistische Strömungen', *Amt und Gemeinde* 67 (2017), 4, 269 283.
16. See the remarkable argument in the *Instruction Erga migrantes caritas Christi* of the Pontifical Council for the Pastoral Care of Migrants and Itinerant People (2004), section 17: 'Foreigners are also a visible sign and an effective reminder of that universality which is a constituent element of the Catholic Church.' http://www.vatican.va/roman_curia/pontifical_councils/migrants/documents/rc_pc_migrants_doc_20040514_erga-migrantes-caritas-christi_en.html
17. Felix Wilfred, 'Asian Approaches to Catholicity. Some Theological Reflections in the Context of Post-Christianity', in *Theological Explorations. Centennial Festschrift in Honour of Josef Neuner S.J.*, Delhi 2008, pp. 173 – 188.
18. In his Post-Synodal Apostolic *Exhortation Ecclesia in Europa* (2003), Pope John-Paul II develops this idea in a very interesting (and extremely provocative) way, which is partuclarly significant in the light of the rebirth of a right-wing populist form of nationalism in Europe. He says: 'the Catholic Church can offer a unique contribution to the building up of a Europe open to the world. The Catholic Church in fact provides a model of essential unity in a diversity of cultural expressions, a consciousness of membership in a universal community which is rooted in but not confined to local communities, and a sense of what unites beyond all that divides' (116): https://w2.vatican.va/content/john-paul-ii/en/apost_exhortations/documents/hf_jp-ii_exh_20030628_ecclesia-in-europa.html
19. Aloys Grillmeier argues that this combination of unity and diversity 'is meant to show that there is room in the people of God for all vocations and ways of life that allow individuals to develop their potential and at the same time benefit the whole. This gives us a catholicity of diversity and the interplay of different orders such that only God's Spirit can tell them apart and also hold them together' (Aloys Grillmeier SJ, Kommentar [Zweites Kapitel], in: *Lexikon für Theologie und Kirche, Das Zweite Vatikanische Konzil. Konstitutionen, Dekrete und Erklärungen. Lateinisch und deutsch. Kommentare*, vol. I, Freiburg im Breisgau, 1966, pp 176-207, quotation from p. 194).
20. In *Adversus haereses* 3.16,6 und 3.22,1-3 Irenaeus of Lyon argues that in his genealogy of Christ (Lk 3.23-38) Luke shows that Jesus 'has recapitulated in himself all the peoples that have been scattered since Adam, including Adam himself' (3.22,2).

The Paradoxes of Populism and the Church's Contribution to Democracy: Some Hypotheses

CARMELO DOTOLO

The hermeneutic conflict started by "populism" sinks its roots in a crisis of democracy, with ambivalent effects such as: the defence of national boundaries; a selective closure of the political and cultural spaces; the marginalisation of the other as stranger-migrant; a prudent revision of the liberal and Western way of life; the re-emergence of connotative "denominational" identity of a precise popular and national belonging. In this framework of reference lies the Church's public responsibility as "people of God" through the care for the ethos of the community; the rights-duties relationship at the service of fraternity; the dialogic exercise between cultures and religions; an economy attentive to integral ecology.

I Democracy and populism: a hermeneutical conflict
It is not at all logical to define the peculiarity of populism, beyond the fact of whether or not it represents a sort of ideological *brand* concerning the opposition between the (corrupt) *elite* and the (pure) people, on the basis of a moral vision of politics. It seems to interpret a new line of "fundamental divide" within the contemporary socio-political and cultural framework. Such a *cleavage* appears to be a radical crisis-creation of processes which, over in time have constructed the architecture of public space, where cognitive models and ethical practices mark out a *process of de-democratisation*[1] which seems to erode the intentionality of an appropriate relationship between state action and the questions of its citizens. If contemporary history can be read within a gradual democratic

path, nevertheless in it the principle of modern subjectivity has colluded with cultural, social, religious and ethical elements which have attempted a more or less balanced configuration of the anthropological and social aspects. One cannot disregard the path of freedom and emancipation which modernity represents in promoting a different image of the world and a liberal culture. In this sense, the *symbolism of human rights* constitutes a valuable semantic perspective, one whose structural principles, which place the human person and his / her dignity as referent of every hermeneutic of political and social action, cannot be revised. Nevertheless, the emphasis on the autonomy of the subject and on the deployment of his / her decision-making self-referentiality has resulted in a distortion in the reading of the democratic paths, enabling the construction of a transparent society devoid of conflicts. Christianity itself, carrier of democratic models and of an open humanism, has not always been able to how to offer a critical discernment of the contribution of its message to the cultural change taking place with regard to histories of inequality and marginalisation.

Should not the church, which places itself at the point of intersection between rich and poor nations, here become the fearless *lobby* of these poor nations, for their right to take part in the decisions of world politics, for equality in questions of human rights and against the dominant opinion that the assumptions about people's rights in truth represent imperatives which, in the commercial world, are alien to the system?[2]

Globalisation has in fact engendered populist ideology in replacing the sources of the socio-cultural processes, on the one hand building the market, on the other, science and technology, as key to understanding reality. The decisive corollary is the re-formulation of values such as freedom and democracy as derivatives of the most persuasive cultural codices which, in the figure of the *network* as a socio-economic paradigm, have brought about a crisis of the public space through the influence of neoliberal myths. The hypothesis of a *post-democratic* (and cyber-democratic) form of contemporary social reality is bringing out the ambiguous fascination of a "real democracy" which, while it guarantees the centrality of the new citizen/client, at the same time configures the citizen/client as passive beneficiary of a political spectacle and the place for calculating the balance of power between political (and economic) decision-makers and the media.

II. Populism, a *sui generis* chapter in political theology?

The need to identify a *leit-motiv* in the semantic constellation of populism must take into account the problematic nature of the category people, in relation to which populism is a constructive mode of its appearance. Without doubt, it refers to the question of the form and idea of representative democracy and presents itself as the vehicle of more direct participation in society. In the face of an exacerbation of the institutionalisation of democracy, populism describes a democracy of the people, of ordinary people, suggesting a different and more involved public experience without party mediation and, above all, one which is closer to the daily concerns, the need for security, defence of traditional identities, the demand for an adequate *welfare state*. In other words, it acts as a spokesperson for ethical questions, relying on a uniformity of tradition and on a substratum of religious adherence inspired by a certain post-liberal theology. How can that not be seen in the populist offer of democracy, on a homogeneous background representative of people or nation, through identification with a leader who reveals an ideal and / or a claim of pure democracy? From such a point of view, populism would be a 'chapter of political theology which brings us to the foundations of democratic supremacy, where it sinks its roots: the interpretation of the people and majority rule'.[3] In the end, the wilfulness of populism emerges in the proposal of the re-shaping of the social framework within a logic of returning the processes of globalisation, deemed violent and expropriating of identity, to the local level. In particular, it makes itself a champion of the defence of national boundaries; of the selective closure of the geopolitical and cultural spaces; of the marginalisation of the other as foreigner-migrant; of a prudent revision of the liberal and Western *way of life*; of the re-emergence of the connotative denominational identity of a precise popular and national adherence.

III Epistemological premise: Church and public space

The current cultural circumstances seem to open a renewed space for dialogue between civil and religious institutions. It should benefit democracy with its illustrative principles. But, above all, a different attention is being focussed on the design of a shared *ethos*, a space for critical debate and indications of a path suitable for the demands of history and social and environmental problems. In particular, the Church can work towards a view of inter-society learning based not on a standardised cultural inheritance, nor on a model of people-*ethnos*, but on a new vision of citizenship attentive to persons and their dignity. Christianity is invited to show the reasons for its expertise with regard to the construction of the public space, starting a discussion warning about the drift from an ideological reading of populisms as an alternative to democratic processes. Essentially, this refers back to the Church's task as a socio-cultural *partnership* able to undertake critically a 'the desacralization of the state, the relativization of forms of political order, and the democratization of political decisions'.[4] To inhabit the shared space therefore implies laying out paths of liberation in terms of secular productiveness and assistance in the itineraries of social democratisation. That is to say: in favour of a fundamental equality, complete participation, universal justice, promotion of *radical qualitative* needs on the basis of the theoretical and ethical priority of the dignity of the human person.

A consequence is that the purpose of the church institution is that of being a metaphor for a different world, in which the logic of fraternity and dialogue outlines a *critical humanism* in which the culture of human rights is combined with that of the right of peoples. The alternative nature of ecclesial communities lies in their capacity to translate the symbolic community as indicator of a different life style. In this sense, the Church's potential to undertake a critical distancing from populist forms of reading the social-cultural reality is part of its self-understanding, boosted by the event of Vatican II. From it emerged *a difference in the liberal idea of democracy* which criticises the neo-liberalist cultural and economic ideal; it *opposes* an *absolutisation of every power*, according to the fact that any form of authority is never self-referential, but at the service of the community; it proposes *a representation of minorities*, against the risk that the majority principle is transformed into a tyranny of the majority; it identifies in the exercise of *human rights* a paradigm shift in relations between the religious and the secular, in that there is reference to the ethical construction of the person and his / her historical responsibility in the search for the common good. From this dual premise it is possible to trace some outline of a possible ecclesial contribution to a critical reading of the neo-populist position.

IV The Christian *Weltanschaaung* for a new narrative of the world and of society

In order to understand the ecclesial contribution to the populist question it is appropriate to read its intentionality within a certain idea of society and culture. If populism signals a *deficit* of democratic *governance*, nevertheless it uses such criticism in a surreptitious manner, since it uses the democratic process precisely to subvert it.[5] This is not so much according to a *global polity*, but along the lines of principles such as popular sovereignty and national autonomy. This option acts on the conviction that democracy's natural *habitat* is the State, where the self-determination of the freedom of a people, its denominational identity, its values tied to forms of 'civil religion', takes place. Now, such a vision of the State as territorial and cultural glue must take into account a process of constant change in its shape and gradual adjustments which have some implications and not a few contradictions. Inter alia, the re-discovery of the limitations on immigration which is deemed to be unacceptable, which is of importance so that territory is an indicator of belonging and criterion to discern which civil, economic and social rights are of worth and which are not; the fragility of the representative democracies of States, which must mitigate the sharing of its tasks with supranational entities which impose *diktats* which often clash with the possibility of life and development for all; the risk of a religious-roots rhetoric such as the claim of an identity closed to suitable cultural creation. Such complexity merges into the question of whether a multicultural model of society organisation, whose affirmative hypothesis functions alongside the culture of the principles of community and the common good which belongs to the experience of the Church's "Catholicity", is feasible or not. In this framework is found the theological-ecclesial contribution which is laid out in: a) *care for the ethos of the community*; b) *in the rights-duties relationship at the service of fraternity*; c) *in the dialogic exercise between cultures and religions*; d) in *an economy attentive to integral ecology.*

a) Care for the ethos of the community.
In the architecture of Christian thought the recognition of the centrality of the human person and the care of the *ethos* of the community constitute a hermeneutical viewpoint aimed at a different socio-cultural configuration. If the personalist principle which led to the constitution of the dignity

of the human person dominates in the space of rights, the defence of the common good for the very idea of political and social community is more sensitively outlined. The reason lies in the possibility of identifying a *code of understanding and coexistence* which rises from the hegemonic prerogative of a culture and has universal intentionality. Beyond the conflict between communitarians and neo-liberals, the identification of the community principle on the part of Christianity ends in the *onto-ethical code of recognition*, a code which is feasible because it assumes the whole of existence. In the democractic-community spirit such a code affirms the equality of all in reciprocity of recognition, where the universal needs of freedom and dignity can boost a political life in which communitarian claims are not just about the subjective good, but also the *right* which changes the epistemological status of one's own affinities, beliefs, or life plans. According to the ecclesiological perspective of the 'people of God', the community principle, while highlighting the insufficiency of individual autonomy within a relational dynamic, leads to the importance of the community as a space of mutual and developmental learning, where the style of consultation and deliberation can contribute to the growth of responsibility in respect of differences. In such a process, the church *leadership* itself can encourage the growth and care of the communities so that they become 'hermeneutical communities', capable of generating indicative criteria and life practices that are socially constructive in the logic of the *cultural diaconia*.

b) In the rights-duties relationship at the service of fraternity.
If it is true that the community principle calls us to be open to the common good, to the care of relationships, where the criterion of justice and dignity goes beyond any evaluation of an ideological or ethnic nature or gender, one can understand the populist ideological straining of the distorted reading of the other. Under the pretext of ethnic settings and cultural identities with unmistakable roots lies the hidden symptom of a disruptive dynamic which characterises developed societies and the conditions of well-being of a status quo deemed to be unchangeable. Racial prejudice, xenophobic violence and consequent hostility reject the change which is suggested by socio-cultural metamorphosis, in the conviction that interculturality is impossible, a useless and illusory excess about the possibility of creating forms of coexistence.[6] Under such an appearance, the inter-

cultural vocation of Christianity indicates the assumption of the other as the interpretative place of the *humana conditio*, especially if the other is a stranger or a migrant. The typology offered by the biblical text is enlightening: the other is impoverished, the orphan, the widow, the enemy, figures who deconstruct the solidity of a self-sufficient culture and invite one to leave behind neutrality and indifference. The very style of Jesus Christ establishes a new human and social reality, re-interpreting every organic conception of the relationship with the other and bringing it to its saturation point: before the other who does not belong to my group, who is foreign in his or her cultural and religious particularity, the encounter which occurs can only be analogous to the *inaugural gesture* of the gift as *paradoxical law of existence*. This law means going beyond the subject in the interest of the other, to the point of taking his or her place, as the *paradigm of the Samaritan* shows, so that a conviviality of differences can begin.

In such a perspective, the same affirmation of human rights necessitates not just a broadening to cultural, social, and religious rights, but a semantic development which recognises the other as a limit and condition of freedom and turns attention to the *right-need* relationship, rather than right-capacity. It is precisely in this connection that Christianity sees a different and maieutic universality of rights, which necessarily tend towards solidarity, inscribed in the welcome of the other as the one who is in need. From this point of view, the Christian perspective nourishes the ethic of rights through that of *duty*. Here, then is a real paradox: the affirmation of rights finds its ethical and political value in the discovery of duty towards others, towards whom I am called to responsibility and solidarity. It is not surprising, therefore, that in the biblical text duty is outlined as an inter-subjective, community, and social right, which ranges from not harming the rights of the weakest (cf. Deut 24:17-22) to the care, responsibility for and welcome of others (cf. Matt 25). The true ethical strength of human rights is expressed when the rights of the weak, of victims, and of the marginalised are placed at the centre. From this perspective, the phenomenology of rights certainly appeals to liberty, but by virtue of *fraternity*. Without this condition, it is difficult to combine individual rights with social, religious, economic, and ecological ones.

c) In the exercise of dialogue between cultures and religions.

And yet, learning a way of being open to the other cannot avoid the mention of a latent prejudice concerning a cultural diversity which invites different educative processes. To encounter another culture and religion is an event which enables the subject to see a thought different from their own, sometimes, though not often, divergent. It seems evident that the success or otherwise of a process of inter-culturality also depends on the ability of religions *to live the exercise of dialogue*. In fact, to assume it as an ethical challenge, by virtue of the historico-social responsibility they have as constellations of meaning which are not indifferent to the construction of life. In particular, religions attest to "Another reality" which enlarges the value space and offers a cultural critical hermeneutic concerning those self-referential and exclusive historical experiences. To establish an ethical dialogue at the inter-religious level means creating the minimum conditions for a stimulus to reciprocity, whose authenticity can be achieved as interpretation and change. Dialogue between religions, in fact, has the historical task of demolishing the incompatibility between symbolically different universes, directing the antagonistic trend towards relations which promote peace and justice on a planetary scale.[7] The principle of religious freedom and equality, expressed in the individual's potential to live and change their own identity and belonging, is no longer sufficient, even if it is decisive. A new style of co-operation between states and religions is required, not only where religious communities are better integrated into the cultural and social tradition of a people. It is true that a strong question of identity and of symbols in which one can recognise oneself, where religion represents an important stock of values on which to draw, have emerged from the profound crisis of transformation in recent years. The attention focussed on the social, cultural and political dimensions of religion must therefore include all religions, otherwise there is a risk of re-creating ideological blocs and discrimination between strong and rooted religious groups and new religious movements, religious minorities and other religions.

d) In an economy attentive to integral ecology.
Finally, according to what has been said, the theological perspective of human rights understood as duties of solidarity, calls into question some assumptions of the liberal-individualist theory of rights, according to which the attribution of those rights is linked to the individual process of

pursuing one's own interests, deeming the dynamic of social interaction to be irrelevant. The preference for one's own interest works on a commercial conception of socio-economic culture, sowing the conviction that a happy life characterised by well-being can be found in openness to the indiscriminate use of resources and the decisive motivational basis in their financial yield. In fact, that does not contradict the potentiality of the economy, but its monetary rendition. However, the globalisation of the market opens out scenarios of standardised and homogeneous consumption which pervades life styles, under the cloak of the indefinite accumulation of monetary assets. It is at this level of the problem that it becomes evermore critical for Christianity to propose the *ethical-cultural value of the economy* as a place of development and freedom. The logic of infinite quantitative growth, in fact, is creating a new collective image, that of competitiveness, acceleration and efficiency which, at the social level, decides on the functionality of work and the adequacy of social activity.[8] Acting as arbitrator is *the law of the market* which, managing cash flow, evaluates how the financial mechanism can jam, deciding to eliminate those distortions which cause friction in the mechanism of production in the accumulation of capital. But, more seriously, a subtle dynamism has been triggered in the re-reading of human rights, in which the *rights of the owner* are stirring in the background. The on-going transformation is obvious, especially in the advancement of dramatic paradoxes: wider social discrimination; a capitalist raid on the environment; increasing signs of malaise such as depression, obesity, and the global *crisis burn out*; increase in the *per capita* GDP and growth in debt among families, faced with the difficulties of being able to pay for public goods such as education and health. From this perspective, the cultural responsibility of the Church's social teaching can lead to a more articulated reflection on the economic and ethical relationship, on the basis of the principles of *co-operation* and *subsidiarity*. It suggests that the economy of relations and social cohesion are decisive in the logic of an *economic democracy*,[9] as it can realise a global market in which to work in conditions of legal and economic-financial parity. Avoiding discrimination, it is possible to recover the idea of co-operative enterprises, according to an *economy of communion* which places at the centre a different culture of efficiency, no longer focussed on profit, but on the opportunity to create work, and for those carrying handicaps, too. A consequence is a social quality of markets which is reflected on a model of *enabling welfare*, no longer a dependency, based on the need dimension of the human condition. But the salient element means shaping *new life styles*, changing the perspective of irresponsible consumerism towards critical forms of attention to saving, to sharing, to sobriety, in such a way that needs can be satisfied, reducing the use of resources and production of waste to a minimum. That is possible if the common good becomes a condition for a cultural conversion aimed at an *integral ecological vision*, as testified by Pope Francis' *Laudato Si'*.

V Non-conclusive gloss: heterotopia of the people of God

It is not out of place to speculate that Christianity's undeniable contribution is to work on behalf of a *conviviality of differences*. This task, which demands of the Church that it be a *community of meaning* as intermediary institution between people and societies, is not an easy one. The theoretical and ethical strength of its life style now come into play: to live the logic of fraternity, to bring about forms of solidarity, to develop a critique of social injustices and inequalities, to shape a democratic culture at the service of the least and the marginalised. In this sense it takes on reality as the symbolic 'people of God' spreads in the church of the poor, which places at its centre the principle of compassion and the hermeneutic of history starting from those who are suffering and impoverished. Here the future proclamation of the promise of liberation is possible, because 'the church institution is in effect the public carrier of a promise. Without this originality, its role and its witness collapse'.[10]

Translated by Patricia Kelly

Notes

1. According to C. Tilly, *La democrazia*, Bologna, Il Mulino, 2009, p. 81-115, the democratic crisis occurs if there is a weakening between three fundamental processes: the integration of the fiduciary networks; the neutralisation of the inequalities of category; the elimination of the centres of autonomous power. Cf. Y. Mounk, *Popolo vs Democrazia. Dalla cittadinanza alla dittatura elettorale*, Milan, Feltrinelli, 2018, p. 178-195.
2. J.B. Metz, *Memoria passionis. Un ricordo provocatorio nella società pluralista*, Brescia, Queriniana, 2009, p. 190.
3. N. Urbinati, *Un termine abusato, un fenomeno controverso*, in J-W. Müller, *Cos'è il populismo?*, Milan, Università Bocconi Editore, 2017, p. xvii.
4. J. Moltmann, *God for a secular society*. Trans. Margaret Kohl. London, SCM Press, p. 44. Cf. S. Kim, *Theology in The Public Sphere: Public Theology as a Catalyst for Open*

Debate, London, SCM Press, 2011.
5. Cf. H. Geiselberger (ed.), *La grande regressione. Quindici intellettuali da tutto il mondo spiegano la crisi del nostro tempo*, Milan, Feltrinelli, 2018.
6. T. Todorov, *I nemici intimi della democrazia*, Milan, Garzanti, 2012, p. 179-220 underlines the demagogical prominence of populism which takes its chances on an emotional identity. Xenophobic rejection is a sign of an inability to look beyond the present, in ignorance of points of view, conflicts of interest, of the heterogeneity of society.
7. Cf. H. Küng, *Etica mondiale per la politica e l'economia*, Brescia, Queriniana, 2002, p. 248-264.
8. Cf. H. Rosa, *Accelerazione e alienazione: per una teoria critica del tempo nella tarda modernità*, Turin, Einaudi, 2015.
9. Cf. S. Zamagni, *L'economia del bene comune*, Rome, Città Nuova, 2007, p. 122-147.
10. C. Duquoc, *«Credo la Chiesa». Precarietà istituzionale e Regno di Dio*, Brescia, Queriniana, 2001, p. 326. Cf. J. Sobrino, "A critique and unmasking of present-day democracies and ways of humanizing them from the biblical-Jesuanic tradition", *Concilium* 43 (2007/4), p. 91-107.

Part Four: Theological Forum

Summer of Shame: American Catholics and the Latest Wave of the Abuse Crisis

CATHLEEN KAVENY

A new wave of the clergy sex abuse crisis has crashed upon the American shore, prompting unprecedented levels of anguish and disgust among Catholics in the United States. Some commentators have wondered, why now? What is different about this wave? After all, it is not as if anything truly new has appeared. We have long known that about five to seven percent of the priests in the U.S. have abused minors, generally but not always adolescent boys. We have long realized that their episcopal superiors have covered up their behaviour, frequently reassigning them to a new parish after a short stint in a rehabilitation facility. And we understand that the rates of abuse have been sharply reduced since 2002, when the U.S. bishops adopted a number of stringent protective and reporting measures.

So what accounts for the current levels of pain and outrage? In my view, the latest wave of the crisis has prompted many American Catholics to undergo what the philosopher of science Thomas S. Kuhn has called a 'paradigm shift' in their view of the Church.[1] Recent revelations have forced many Catholics in the pews to radically re-frame how they interpret the events that have taken place. Rather than seeing it as an aberration, which can be fixed, they are now beginning to see it as an intrinsic and possibly ineradicable part of the global Catholic culture.

I The Clergy Sex Abuse Crisis in the American Catholic Consciousness

How did American Catholics get to this point? While there had been prior incidents of abuse that received some publicity,[2] the clergy sex abuse crisis in the Catholic Church truly exploded in the American consciousness in 2001, when the *Boston Globe*'s Spotlight team broke the story about serial sex abuser and former diocesan priest John J. Geoghan, then on trial in Massachusetts for sexual assault.[3] It boggled the reader's mind that priests like John Geoghan could sexually assault young children. Even more troubling, however, was the fact that members of the hierarchy like Cardinal Bernard Law had covered up and even enabled such abuse.

The 2001 crisis began to abate after the U.S. Conference of Catholic Bishops adopted the 'Charter for the Protection of Children and Young People' in Dallas, Texas in September 2002.[4] They also commissioned a third-party report (the 'John Jay Report') that allowed everyone to get a better sense of the problem.[5] Over the past fifteen years, the Church in the United States slowly began to heal. The laity developed the sense that the bishops understood the problem, the victims were being treated justly, and the newly implemented reforms were effective. We had the sense that the worst was behind us. Active lay Catholics began to turn our attention to other things.

II Summer of Shame

That sense of relative peace and slow progress was shattered by two events that occurred the summer of 2018. In June, news broke that Theodore McCarrick, the former Cardinal Archbishop of Washington DC, had been removed from public ministry after being credibly abused of molesting a teenager nearly five decades ago while serving as a priest in New York.[6] The next month brought a new set of allegations against the Cardinal, which claimed that he sexually harassed adult seminarians under his authority.[7] A second big blow to American Catholics came in August. The Attorney General of Pennsylvania released the report of a two-year grand jury investigation of six of the eight Pennsylvania dioceses.[8] It showed that over a seventy year period, 301 priests were accused of sexually abusing more than 1,000 children, mostly boys, in the six dioceses. When their crimes became known, they were moved to another parish, rather than removed from the priesthood or reported to the authorities.[9] Both of these blows were exacerbated by a splenetic attack on Pope Francis's handling of the sex abuse situation penned by Carlo Maria Viganò, the former apostolic nuncio to the United States, with the help of a conservative Italian journalist opposed to Francis's program of reform.[10]

Despite the fact that Viganò's case quickly unravelled,[11] American conservatives seized upon him to help promote their interpretation of the crisis: they claimed that its root cause was a culture of rampant homosexuality in the Church. More progressive Catholics, in contrast, accepted the John Jay Report's conclusion that the root cause was not homosexual priests. Instead they saw the problem as rampant clericalism. Ordinary Catholics in the pews, who had not read either the John Jay Report or the Vigano letter, were caught in the crossfire. The sex abuse crisis fuelled the polarization among American Catholics, which both reflected and fed the polarization in American society at large prompted by the Trump presidency.

Moreover, the events of the summer of 2018 were not interpreted by American Catholics in isolation. It had by now become clear that clergy sexual abuse of minors was a global problem. International news revealed wave after wave of clergy sexual abuse and misconduct around the world, in Australia, Chile, France, Germany, Ireland, and other countries.

III A Troubling Paradigm Shift

Some commentators have wondered why the events of the summer of 2018 – the summer of shame – have precipitated such existential anguish among American Catholics. After all, careful scrutiny of the Pennsylvania Grand Jury Report did not reveal anything that had not been unearthed by the John Jay Report fifteen years earlier. Moreover, the Pennsylvania Grand Jury Report reported a sharp drop-off in credible accusations after 2002, when the Dallas norms went into effect. So in some ways, the news is good.

In my view, asking the question in such a manner leads down the wrong path. Recent events are not significant because they added more data to be absorbed by the American Catholic populace. Instead, they matter because they caused a drastic shift in the way that data is organized and understood. They precipitated what Thomas Kuhn calls a 'paradigm shift,' roughly analogous to the shift from a Ptolemaic to a Copernican way of viewing the universe.

Until 2018, many ordinary Catholics saw the crisis as a terrible but ultimately manageable problem. It involved a very small number of disturbed clergy. Their secretive and twisted activities were enabled by overly naïve bishops who wrongly believed them to be cured, or overly cowardly bishops who did not want to bring shame to the Church by exposing their crimes. In this interpretive frame, the clergy sex abuse crisis was essentially a problem of psycho-sexual sickness and/or immaturity (on the part of the offending priests) and moral weakness (on the part of the offending bishops). While undeniably abhorrent, the problem could be solved by better screening and formation in the seminaries, more rigorous reporting and accountability on the part of the hierarchy, and utter transparency about successes and failures.

But now, many American Catholics are beginning to read the very same data in a quite different manner. As much as they would like to believe to the contrary, they are coming to see the child sex abuse crisis not as an aberration, but as a manifestation of something both terrible and fundamental about the character of the Church. Catholics who experience themselves as undergoing this paradigm shift find themselves confronting a deeply threatening question. *If the patterns of sexual abuse they have seen are not an aberration, but are instead an expected, tolerated, and even accepted part of the operation, what else has to be true about the Church?* There are several possible answers to that question, but they all boil down to one appalling insight: Jesus Christ has nothing to do with the life of the Church. It is not, actually, his body. Priests and bishops act in his name, and invoke his authority, but never actually behave in the manner Jesus acts in the Gospels.

IV Grappling with the New Paradigm

American Catholics are losing heart. They may be losing their faith, not necessarily in Jesus Christ, but in the Roman Catholic Church as the Body of Christ, as community that offers communion with the divine. In the best of time, fostering confidence in the importance of the Church's role is problematic, because American culture is so thoroughly permeated by an individualistic account of faith that reflects its Protestant heritage. Addressing the latest wave of the crisis will require grappling with the challenges posed by this paradigm shift. What will this involve?

New procedures of dealing with abuse claims that are characterized by rigour, transparency, and accountability are an important part of the solution – but they are only part of it. Reforming the culture of the church to incorporate more respect and cooperation between clergy and laity is part of the solution – but again, only part of it. Articulating the requirements of just relationships between the powerful and the vulnerable is also part of the solution, but just a part of it as well. A lasting and comprehensive response, it seems to me, will require grappling with the emerging paradigm produced by the summer of shame. That will be a task not only for lawyers and ethicists, but also for systematic theologians, ecclesiologists, and liturgists.

More specifically, I think that addressing the theological and ecclesiological aspects of the crisis is necessary if any legal, moral, and cultural responses are to be effective in the long run. One necessary change will cut deep. Catholic theologians have long taught that the Church, as the bride of Christ, was sinless, without spot or stain. Individual members of the Church could and did sin – but those sins were their own fault, and could not be attributed to the collective body. Addressing this crisis adequately will require the Church to rethink this position. Just as Germany had to take collective responsibility for the atrocities of the Third Reich, and the United States still must grapple with its collective responsibility for slavery, so too the Church must take collective responsibility for the sex abuse crisis. That will require some hard theological and ecclesiological reflection about the ways in which the Church is the Whore of Babylon—not merely the Bride of Christ.

Notes

1. Thomas S. Kuhn, *The Structure of Scientific Revolutions*, 3rd ed. (Chicago, IL: University of Chicago Press, 1996).
2. The first highly publicized clergy sex abuse case broke open in the 1990's; it involved former priest James R. Porter. See, e.g., Alison Bass, 'Nine Allege Priest Abused Them, Threaten to Sue Church,' *Boston Globe*, May 8, 1992, http://archive.boston.com/globe/spotlight/abuse/archives/050892_porter.htm.
3. Michael Rezendes et al. (the Globe Spotlight team), 'Church Allowed Abuse by Priest for Years: Aware of Geoghan Record, Archdiocese Still Shuttled Him from Parish to Parish,' *Boston Globe*, January 6, 2002 (part 1); and Sacha Pfeiffer et al (the Globe Spotlight team), 'Goeghan Preferred Preying on Poorer Children,' *Boston Globe*, January 7, 2002 (part 2).
4. United States Conference of Catholic Bishops, 'Promise to Protect, Pledge to Heal: Charter for the Protection of Children and Young People, Essential Norms for Diocesan/Eparchial Policies Dealing with Allegations of Sexual Abuse of Minors by Priests or Deacons, and A Statement of Episcopal Commitment' (rev. June 2018), http://www.usccb.org/issues-and-action/child-and-youth-protection/upload/Charter-for-the-Protection-of-Children-and-Young-People-2018-final.pdf.
5. United States Conference of Catholic Bishops, 'The Nature and Scope of Sexual Abuse

of Minors by Catholic Priests and Deacons in the United States 1950–2002 (the 'John Jay Report'), June 2002, http://www.usccb.org/issues-and-action/child-and-youth-protection/upload/The-Nature-and-Scope-of-Sexual-Abuse-of-Minors-by-Catholic-Priests-and-Deacons-in-the-United-States-1950-2002.pdf.

6. Laurie Goodstein and Sharon Otterman, 'American Cardinal Accused of Sexually Abusing Minor Is Removed From Ministry,' *New York Times*, June 20, 2018, ://www.nytimes.com/2018/06/20/us/theodore-mccarrick-sex-abuse.html.

7. Laurie Goodstein and Sharon Otterman, 'He Preyed on Men Who Wanted to Be Priests. Then He Became a Cardinal,' *New York Times*, July 16, 2018, https://www.nytimes.com/2018/07/16/us/cardinal-mccarrick-abuse-priest.html.

8. Attorney General of Pennsylvania, 'Pennsylvania Diocese Victims Report' (August 14, 2018), https://www.attorneygeneral.gov/report/.

9. Alex Johnson, 'After Shocking Catholic Abuse Report, the Law Can Do Little—For Now,' NBC News, August 15, 2018, https://www.nbcnews.com/storyline/sexual-misconduct/after-shocking-catholic-abuse-report-law-can-do-little-now-n900786.

10. Jason Horowitz, 'The Man Who Took On Pope Francis: The Story Behind the Viganò Letter,' *New York Times*, August 28, 2018, https://www.nytimes.com/2018/08/28/world/europe/archbishop-carlo-maria-vigano-pope-francis.html.

11. See, e.g., Laurie Goodstein and Jason Horowitz, 'If Cardinal Was Under Pope's Sanctions, Why Was He Allowed at Gala Events?,' *New York Times*, September 1, 2018, https://www.nytimes.com/2018/09/01/world/europe/pope-francis-benedict-mccarrick.html.

Listening to the Conversation: After the Synod of Bishops Meeting on Young People, the Faith and Vocational Discernment

BRUNO CADORÉ

Placing this recent synod in the arc of the two previous ones (on evangelization and on the family), Pope Francis intended to insist particularly that it should be an example of the synodical process by which the Church is built and lives. This idea governed the process employed to prepare the synod – not just the questionnaires normally sent to local churches, but also an online questionnaire, regional meetings and a pre-synod meeting with representatives of young people from around the world. It was essential to use all possible means to listen to young people in their diversity, just as it was important that as many representatives of young people as possible should be invited to be present at the synod and speak. Listening to young people was an essential objective because this was to be a sort of starting-point, and perhaps a criterion by which the synod's work was to be assessed.

At the heart of this synodical process, the voice of these young people was analogous to the question asked by the youngest member of the group celebrating the paschal *seder* in the Jewish tradition: 'Why is this night like no other night?' he or she asks the person presiding at the celebration. And the presider recounts once more the memorial narrative of the liberation of the people by which that people was formed, established and sent into the world as a people chosen by God. Something like this was perhaps the situation of the young people invited to the synod: through their ideas and the questions they asked their Church, they invited that Church to express with them, once again, but perhaps in a fresh way, what the Church wished to be and become, and what it wished to be and become with them. Here the term 'conversation' is completely apposite, especially in relation to a synod at which the canonisation of Pope Paul VI was celebrated, the pope who insisted so much that the Church, the Church whose essence is evangelization, should become dialogue and conversation, internally and in the world. So evangelization through conversation is the mark of a synod.

There is another young person, like the one at the paschal *seder*, in St John's gospel (Jan 6.5-15). Jesus is discussing with Philip and the other disciples, who are worried about how to feed so many people. Andrew has found a boy who may not have much with him, but offers it generously. And his presence, his offering, allows Jesus, with his disciples, to begin the adventure of the mission of communion. At root, for the Church today the task of the synod was perhaps to be listening to these two young people, the one at the paschal meal and the one at the sea of Tiberias, and to be guided by them to say what it is and to put that identity into practice with their resources and with them. This is how we have to understand the synod's call now to the particular churches, the religious and spiritual traditions, and all groups in the Church, to continue, extend and bring to fruition this conversation with young people; the final document is only the 'progress report' of a wider adventure that calls on the Church to discover itself.

I Three key elements of the synod conversation
From this conversation at the synod we can pick out three important 'elements' of a new collective awareness. The first is the realisation that it was really impossible, and would not have been appropriate, to consider 'the young people of the world' as a single category, so great is the diversity among them. Nonetheless it became very clear that, in that diversity, the young people showed themselves to be pointers to the big questions, the principal changes and the fault lines in our contemporary worlds. This was the case with many of the topics the synod took an interest in: intercultural relationships, the diversity of socio-economic situations, the great diversity of the world of work and the difficulty of getting access to it, the important phenomenon of migration, whether for political reasons or for reasons of extreme poverty in ordinary everyday

life, immersion in the digital world – especially the area of social media – the violence and injustice of wars, situations of religious persecution. Beginning a conversation with young people today means listening to the experiences of these sufferings, these breakdowns, and of the hopes that, despite everything, persist.

A second element was the insistence, by several speakers in the plenary and also by several working groups, on the fact that the community should have an essential role in any process of accompaniment or discernment. This is a crucial issue for the preparation for the future of the Church. It is not possible to consider young people in an 'inter-individual' perspective, still less when that could produce the result of mutual discouragement. On the contrary, the Christian community must discover ways of strengthening its attractiveness, of becoming a place where each person can nourish his or her own human life, their faith, their moral thinking.... In short, the community is the place where a brother or sister must be able to mature and to make this possible the communities must make it their aim to 'nourish the lives of each one of their members'. The various young people of the world, each in their own way, are marked by very radical mutations in the way the post-modern individual relates to the human community. This realisation should lead the Church to rethink the place given to the community, to the development communities as places to which people want to belong.

A third element was thinking about the interaction required between accompaniment and discernment. Reading the working document might give the impression that the dynamic proposed was the following: discern the vocations and after that think about what would be the most appropriate accompaniment. In reality life in the Church is very different, since the Church can't be thought of or understood as a juxtaposition of individual persons who require support once their needs have been discerned. The Church is called to bear witness as a community of faith, of belonging, of mission, and it is through being all these things that the community 'accompanies' its members. By walking with them, becoming companions, the Church is built up and makes itself available for the Spirit to make it 'mission'. This point of view of the mission is a criterion and a support for a process of discernment through dialogue with people. But it is also the point of view from which the Church itself must constantly discern how far it is responding to the call to mission, the call to live in a permanent state of mission.

II Three underlying questions

The conversation at the synod was marked by three questions very much in the minds of all the participants, even if they were not all explicitly discussed to the same degree by the assembly.

The first question was the distress and contrition of the Church in the face of the extremely serious scandal of the abuse of young people of which certain members have been guilty during recent decades, without Church leaders really taking responsibility as they should have done for dealing with these errant or criminal members. The assembly expressed its distress and stated once again, on the one hand that it considered it a priority to pay attention, to listen to and support the people who had suffered these abuses and, on the other, its determination to achieve clarity on the matter and to make every possible effort to ensure that such situations do not recur.

The second question underlying the conversation is about intercultural issues. For this particular synod these came up in the very definition of the group called 'young people': you are not young in the same way, or for as long, if you are student in the North and West or looking after a family from adolescence, as in other contexts. Passing on cultural heritage isn't thought of in the same way in the North and the South, in the East and the West. The nuclear family isn't the obvious family model in all cultures, and the close link between youth and education doesn't take the same form in all latitudes.... The diversity of young people's ties to the Church also needs stressing, from those who are involved and have specific responsibilities to those who are more distant, from those who fully accept the life of the Church as it is today to those who aspire to make connections with older or more classical traditions in liturgy, theology and morality..., between those who have received the faith in a Church deeply engaged in the social and political life of their country, which may often be torn by serious conflict, and those who, on the contrary, believe that the Church should keep its distance from such involvements. This diversity makes the unity of the Church as a communion of one and the same people riven but also formed by intercultural differences.

The third issue is that of synodality, though it should be stressed that the issue wasn't central at the synod and wasn't much mentioned in the discussions between the members. Nevertheless, the issues of accompaniment and communion were very much discussed. This should make us read the insistence on the issue of synodality in the Final Document (and the messaging about it) in connection with the stress placed on accompaniment. This twofold stress expresses the essentially reciprocal character of the experience of communion in the Church. There is reciprocity in accompaniment. Where the synod had perhaps imagined that its task was to discern how to accompany young people today, the bishops discovered that – as with families and their younger members – it was possible to accompany the younger people to the extent that the bishops were prepared to let them accompany the older. Or, to put it a different way, young people in the Church accompany their elders as much as they do them. A child educates a parent, people say, as much as a parent educates a child.

But there is reciprocity as well in synodality. The main thing about synodality is that it illustrates the identity of the Church: it follows the two disciples who had recognised the risen Jesus and the sign of the bread broken and went back to Jerusalem and beyond to proclaim the good news to which they were witnesses. Synodality says that the Church's vocation is to be a companion of the world, a witness to the world's ability to understand God's call and the promise of communion. This missionary synodality is particularly important when to comes to proclaiming to the young generations who are preparing, in their turn, to answer for the world and its vocation to be hospitable to humanity. This where the preferential option for young people takes on its full breadth and force: today is the reality of tomorrow and what makes it possible for tomorrow to be everyone's today. It is to bring this about that the Church today has the duty to recognise and promote the right of the young generation to be leaders in the Church, full actors, in synodical reciprocity, in its mission now.

III Three topics for a continuing conversation with young people

What are the main topics for a conversation that the synod seems to want to continue in the particular churches to make the Church what it is in conversation with the world?

The first is *the reality of communities in the Church*, the communities that make up the Church. In the run-up to the synod, and during it, the young people often expressed regret at not finding this reality sufficiently in the Church. They want to feel at home in the Church, in their own place, welcomed, and in this they essentially express a desire of each and every one of us.

The second topic is *education*. The synod stressed that in many parts of the world the Church had taken on a considerable responsibility for education through its many schools and universities. This fact, which points to the huge and obvious needs in this area, is a call to consolidate and activate existing commitments and strengthen the synergy between the various initiatives with a concern for remedying the inequalities in access to education that represent an injustice for today and a risk of increasing damage to the social fabric tomorrow.

The third topic concerns *the Church's social teaching*. A feature that attracted much attention during the synod was the younger generation's interest in issues that threaten human aspirations to justice, peace, truth and respect for creation. Young people, moreover, are very often the first victims of these situations, with so many conflicts and abuses in the world. Discussing with them, on the basis of their own experience and their aspirations for the future, would place these concerns at the heart of the Church communities to which they belong.

The conclusion of the Final Document turns our eyes towards holiness and importance of the faith community as a support for each member's vocation to holiness. Young people's ideas and appeals to the Church that they want to inhabit as their home, the conversation with them that made it possible to strengthen the reciprocity of our common membership of the Church, all together combined in an appeal to recognise once again the essence of every human being's life – vocation!

Translated by Francis McDonagh

Contributors

MILE BABIĆ (1947) is a Bosnian Franciscan and a professor of theology and philosophy. He graduated in History of Literature; obtained Ph.D.'s in Theology (Christology of Theodoret of Cyrus) and in Philosophy (Hegel's Philosophy of Right). He has been lecturing at the Franciscan Theologate in Sarajevo since 1977. He is the editor-in-chief of *Miscellany Jukic*. The main areas of his research include the Theodoret of Cyrus, John Duns Scotus, Nicolaus Cusanus, G. W. F. Hegel, the contemporary literature, theology and philosophy. Since 2013, he is a member of *Concilium's* editorial board.

Address: Mile Babić OFM, Franjevačka teologija Sarajevo, Aleja Bosne Srebrene 111, BiH-71000 Sarajevo (Bosnia-Herzegovina)
Email: dekan.babic@gmail.com

FRANCIS GONSALVES is an Indian Jesuit, professor of theology, journalist and social activist. Formerly Dean at the Vidyajyoti College of Theology, Delhi, currently Dean of Theology at the Jnana-Deepa Vidyapeeth (JDV), Pune, he is the Executive Secretary of the Catholic Conference of Bishops of India (CCBI) for Theology and Doctrine. He has authored seven books among which are *God of Our Soil: Towards Subaltern Trinitarian Theology* (2010), *Body Broken for Body Building: Christic Living in a Broken Global Village* (2013), *Feet Rooted, Hearts Radiant, Minds Raised: Living Sacraments in India* (2015).

Address: Francis Gonsalves, Jnana-Deepa Vidyapeeth, Ramwadi, Nagar Road, Pune – 411014 (India)
Email: fragons@gmail.com

DILEK SARMIS is a post doctorate fellow in the school of higher studies in social science at the Centre for Turkish, Ottoman, Balkan and Central Asian Studies, (CETOBaC, UMR 8032 EHESS-CNRS). She is the scientific co-ordinator of a Franco–German research project ANR-DFG on the Prophet of Islam and a course leader at INALCO (Institut National

Contributors

des Langues et Civilisations Orientales) in Paris. Author of a doctoral thesis on *La pensée de Bergson dans la genèse de la Turquie moderne. Un prisme des transitions lexicales, institutionnelles et politiques de la fin de l'Empire ottoman à la Turquie républicaine*, she is a specialist in the history of intellect and knowledge of the Ottoman empire and the Turkish Republic and focuses in particular on the history of religious learning.

Address: Dilek SARMIS, ANR-DFG Prophet, Centre d'études turques, ottomanes, balkaniques et centrasiatiques (Cetobac, UMR 8032, CNRS-EHESS), 54, boulevard Raspail, 75006 Paris

Email: dilek.sarmis@gmail.com

FRANÇOIS MABILLE, accredited research supervisor in political science, is a statutory researcher in Religious Groups, societies, lay organisations (CNRS and EPHE Paris) and participates in the work of the International Observatory of religion (Sciences PO-CERI). He is the secretary general of the International Federation of Catholic Universities (FIUC-IFCU). His work centres on Catholic internationalism and the place of religions in international relations.

http://francois-mabille.over-blog.fr/
https://www.gsrl-cnrs.fr/mabille-francois/

Address: François Mabille, Fédération internationale des universités catholiques, 21 rue d'Assas, 75270 – Paris (France)

Email: francois.mabille0702@orange.fr

SUSAN ABRAHAM is Professor of Theology and Postcolonial Cultures, VP of Academic Affairs and Dean of Faculty at Pacific School of Religion. She is the author of *Identity, Ethics, and Nonviolence in Postcolonial Theory: A Rahnerian Theological Assessment* (Palgrave Macmillan, 2007) and co-editor of *Shoulder to Shoulder: Frontiers in Catholic Feminist Theology* (Fortress, 2009). Ongoing research projects include issues in theological education and formation, interfaith and interreligious initiatives for social transformation, theology and political theory, religion and media, global Catholicism, and Christianity between colonialism and postcolonialism.

Address: Susan Abraham, Dean of Faculty, Pacific School of Religion, 1798 Scenic Avenue, Berkeley, CA 94709 (USA)

Email: sabraham@psr.edu

Contributors

MARIDA NICOLACI obtained a Licence in Sacred Scripture from the Pontifical Biblical Institute and a Doctorate in Biblical Theology from the Theology Faculty in Sicily where she currently teaches New Testament Exegesis. Her research is focussed mainly on Johannine Writings and Catholic Epistles, texts considered particulalry representative of the Jewish origins of the Church and of the most Jewish historical and theological traditions in the New Testament.
   Address: Marida Nicolaci, Pontificia Facoltà Teologica di Sicilia 'S. Giovanni evangelista', Via Vittorio Emanuele 463, 90134 Palermo (Italia)
   Email: maridanic@alice.it

ANDREAS LOB-HÜDEPOHL, 67, professor of theological ethics (since 1996) and chief executive of the Berlin Institute for Christian Ethics and Politics, from 1997 to 2011 rector of the Berlin Catholic University for Social Studies and later president of the Catholic University of Eichstätt-Ingolstadt, member of the German Council of Ethics, chair of the Working Group on the Chirch and Right-Wing Populism of the German section of Justitia et Pax, adviser to the pastoral commission of the German Bishops' Conference, and (since 2000) member of the Central Committe of German Catholics.
   Address: Andreas Lob-Hüdepohl, Professor für Theologische Ethik, Katholische Hochschule für Sozialwesen, Köpenicker Allee 39-57, 10318 Berlin (Deutschland)
   Email: andreas.lob-huedepohl@khsb-berlin.de

FRANZ GMAINER-PRANZL, born 1966 in Steyr, Austria, was ordained priest in the diocese of Linz in 1995. After doctorates in theology (Innsbruck) and philosophy (Vienna), he qualified as a professor in fundamental theology at the university of Innsbruck. Since 2009 he has been professor in the Catholic Theology faculty of the university of Salzburg (Austria) and director of the Centre for Intercultural Theology and Study of Religions. His work and resarch is focused principally on intercultural philosophy, doing theology interculturally and the relationships between Africa and Europe. Since 2011 he has been the editor of the series Salzburger interdisziplinäre Diskurse.
   Address: Universität Salzburg, Fachbereich Systematische Theologie, Universitätsplatz 1, A-5020 Salzburg, Austria.
   Email: franz.gmainer-pranzl@sbg.ac.at

Contributors

CARMELO DOTOLO, born in Ariano Irpino (1959), Professor of the Theology of Religions at the Pontificia Università Urbaniana and Dean of the Faculty of Missiology. From 2004-2014 he was President of the Italian Society for Theological Research (SIRT). He is visiting professor at the Univeristy of Urbino, the University of Zara (Croatia), and at the Pontifical Gregorian University. His most recent publications include: L'annuncio del Vangelo. Dal Nuovo Testamento alla Evangelii Gaudium, Cittadella Editrice 2015; Teologia e postcristianesimo. Un percorso interdisciplinare, Queriniana, Brescia 2017.
    Address: Pontificia Università Urbaniana, Via Urbano VIII, 16 – 00165 Roma, Italy
    E-mail: c.dotolo@libero.it

CATHLEEN KAVENY is the Darald and Juliet Libby Professor of Law and Theology at Boston College. She earned her J.D. and her Ph.D. in religious ethics from Yale University. She is the 2018-2019 Cary and Ann Maguire Chair in Ethics and American History at the.Kluge Center at the Library of Congress, where she is working on a book on complicity with wrongdoing. Her most recent book is *Ethics at the Edges of Law: Christian Moralists and American Legal Thought* (Oxford University Press, 2018).
    Address: Cathleen Kaveny, Department of Theology, Boston College, 310 Stokes N, Chestnut Hill, MA 02467
    Email: cathleen.kaveny@bc.edu

BRUNO CADORÉ is a Dominican friar, a medical doctor and a doctor of theology, and a professor of medical ethics. He has been master of the Order of Preachers since 2010, after having been prior provincial of the Dominican province in France. He has published numerous articles and books, especially on bioethical issues, when he was director of the Centre of Medical Ethics at the Institut Catholique of Lille. His latest book is *Avec Lui, écouter l'envers du monde* (Paris, 2018).
    Address: Curia Generalizia Frati Domenicani, Convento Santa Sabina (Aventino), Piazza Pietro d'Illiria, 1, I - 00153 Roma, Italy
    Email: magister@curia.op.org

CONCILIUM
International Journal of Theology

FOUNDERS
Anton van den Boogaard; Paul Brand; Yves Congar, OP; Hans Küng; Johann Baptist Metz; Karl Rahner, SJ; Edward Schillebeeckx

BOARD OF DIRECTORS
President: Thierry-Marie Courau OP
Vice-Presidents: Linda Hogan and Daniel Franklin Pilario CM

BOARD OF EDITORS
Susan Abraham, Los Angeles (USA)
Michel Andraos, Chicago (USA)
Mile Babic' OFM, Sarajevo (Bosna i Hercegovina)
Antony John Baptist, Bangalore (India)
Michelle Becka, Würzburg (Deutschland)
Bernadeth Caero Bustillos, Osnabrück (Deutschland)
Catherine Cornille, Boston (USA)
Thierry-Marie Courau OP, Paris (France)
Geraldo Luiz De Mori SJ, Belo Horizonte (Brasil)
Enrico Galavotti, Chieti (Italia)
Margareta Gruber OSF, Vallendar (Deutschland)
Linda Hogan, Dublin (Ireland)
Huang Po-Ho, Tainan (Zhōnghuá Mínguó)
Stefanie Knauss, Villanova (USA)
Carlos Mendoza-Álvarez OP, Ciudad de México (México)
Gianluca Montaldi FN, Brescia (Italia)
Agbonkhianmeghe Orobator SJ, Nairobi (Kenya)
Daniel Franklin Pilario CM, Quezon City (Filipinas)
Léonard Santedi Kinkupu, Kinshasa (RD Congo)
João J. Vila-Chã SJ, Roma (Italia)

PUBLISHERS
SCM Press (London, UK)
Matthias-Grünewald Verlag (Ostfildern, Germany)
Editrice Queriniana (Brescia, Italy)
Editorial Verbo Divino (Estella, Spain)
EditoraVozes (Petropolis, Brazil)

Concilium Secretariat:
Couvent de l'Annonciation
222 rue du Faubourg Saint-Honoré
75008 – Paris (France)
secretariat.concilium@gmail.com
Executive secretary: Gianluca Montaldi FN

http://www.concilium.in

Concilium Subscription Information

July   2019/3: *Technology: Between Apocalypse and Integration*

October   2019/4: *Christianities and Indigenous Peoples*

December   2019/5: *Queer Theologies: Becoming the Queer Body of Christ*

February   2020/1: *Contextual Theologies Facing the Challenge of Global Violence*

April   2020/2: *Masculinities*

New subscribers: to receive the next five issues of Concilium please copy this form, complete it in block capitals and send it with your payment to the address below. Alternatively subscribe online at www.conciliumjournal.co.uk

Please enter my annual subscription for Concilium starting with issue 2019/3.

Individuals
____ £52 UK
____ £75 overseas and (Euro €92, US $110)

Institutions
____ £75 UK
____ £95 overseas and (Euro €120, US $145)

Postage included – airmail for overseas subscribers

Payment Details:
Payment can be made by cheque or credit card.
a. I enclose a cheque for £/$/€ ____ Payable to Hymns Ancient and Modern Ltd
b. To pay by Visa/Mastercard please contact us on +44(0)1603 785911 or go to www.conciliumjournal.co.uk

Contact Details:
Name ....
Address ....
....
Telephone .... E-mail ....

Send your order to *Concilium,* **Hymns Ancient and Modern Ltd**
13a Hellesdon Park Road, Norwich NR6 5DR, UK
E-mail: concilium@hymnsam.co.uk
or order online at www.conciliumjournal.co.uk

Customer service information
All orders must be prepaid. Your subscription will begin with the next issue of Concilium. If you have any queries or require Information about other payment methods, please contact our Customer Services department.

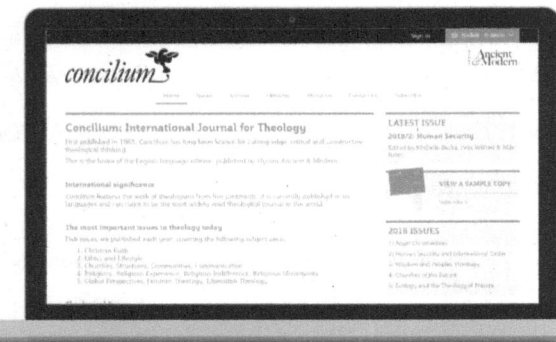

The Canterbury Dictionary of
HYMNOLOGY

The result of over ten years of research by an international team of editors, The Canterbury Dictionary of Hymnology is the major online reference work on hymns, hymn-writers and traditions.

www.hymnology.co.uk

CHURCH TIMES The Church Times, founded in 1863, has become the world's leading Anglican newspaper. It offers professional reporting of UK and international church news, in-depth features on faith, arts and culture, wide-ranging comment and all the latest clergy jobs. Available in print and online.

www.churchtimes.co.uk

Crucible Crucible is the Christian journal of social ethics. It is produced quarterly, pulling together some of the best practitioners, thinkers, and theologians in the field. Each issue reflects theologically on a key theme of political, social, cultural, or environmental significance.

www.cruciblejournal.co.uk

JLS Joint Liturgical Studies offers a valuable contribution to the study of liturgy. Each issue considers a particular aspect of liturgical development, such as the origins of the Roman rite, Anglican Orders, welcoming the Baptised, and Anglican Missals.

www.jointliturgicalstudies.co.uk

magnet Magnet is a resource magazine published three times a year. Packed with ideas for worship, inspiring artwork and stories of faith and justice from around the world.

www.ourmagnet.co.uk

For more information on these publications visit the websites listed above or contact **Hymns Ancient & Modern**:
Tel.: +44 (0)1603 785 910
Write to: Subscriptions, Hymns Ancient & Modern,
13a Hellesdon Park Road, Norwich NR6 5DR